IMPROVING
PERFORMANCE
THROUGH
STATISTICAL THINKING

Also available from ASQ Quality Press

The Quality Audit Handbook, Second Edition
J. P. Russell, editing director

SPC Essentials and Productivity Improvement: A Manufacturing Approach
William A. Levinson and Frank Tumbelty

Mapping Work Processes
Dianne Galloway

Root Cause Analysis: Simplified Tools and Techniques
Bjørn Anderson

Statistical Procedures for Machine and Process Qualification, Third Edition
Edgar Dietrich and Alfred Schulze

Statistical Quality Control Using Excel (with Software)
Steven M. Zimmerman and Marjorie Icenogle

The Certified Quality Manager Handbook
ASQ Quality Management Division

Quality Problem Solving
Gerald F. Smith

To request a complimentary catalog of ASQ Quality Press publications, call 800-248-1946 or visit our Website at qualitypress.asq.org.

IMPROVING PERFORMANCE THROUGH STATISTICAL THINKING

GALEN C. BRITZ
DONALD W. EMERLING
LYNNE B. HARE
ROGER W. HOERL
STUART J. JANIS
JANICE E. SHADE

ASQ Quality Press
Milwaukee, Wisconsin

Improving Performance Through Statistical Thinking

Improving performance through statistical thinking / Galen C. Britz ... [et al.].
    p. cm.
    Includes index.
    ISBN 0-87894-677-
    1. Industrial management—Statistical methods. 2. Industrial management—Statistical methods—Case studies. I. Britz, Galen C., 1939–
    HD30.215 .I47 1999
    658.4'03–dc21   99-046720

10 9 8 7 6 5 4 3 2

ISBN 0-87389-467-7

Acquisitions Editor: Ken Zielske
Production Administrator: Shawn Dohogne
Project Editor: Annemieke Koudstaal

ASQ Mission: The American Society for Quality advances individual and organizational performance excellence worldwide by providing opportunities for learning, quality improvement, and knowledge exchange.

Attention: Bookstores, Wholesalers, Schools and Corporations: ASQ Quality Press books, videotapes, audiotapes, and software are available at quantity discounts with bulk purchases for business, educational, or instructional use. For information, please contact ASQ Quality Press at 800-248-1946, or write to ASQ Quality Press, P.O. Box 3005, Milwaukee, WI 53201-3005.

To place orders or to request a free copy of the ASQ Quality Press Publications Catalog, including ASQ membership information, call 800-248-1946. Visit our web site at www.asq.org or qualitypress.asq.org.

Printed in the United States of America

♾ Printed on acid-free paper

American Society for Quality

Quality Press
611 East Wisconsin Avenue
Milwaukee, Wisconsin 53202
Call toll free 800-248-1946
www.asq.org
qualitypress.asq.org
standardsgroup.asq.org

FOREWORD

Today's business is extremely complex and dynamic. Mergers, downsizing, and acquisitions are commonplace. Companies must quickly understand their ever-changing environments through the use of data and information or face a dismal future.

But how do we collect data and information? There are many texts written on Total Quality Management (TQM), Continuous Improvement (CI) and statistics. The tools and techniques they describe are imperative to understanding data in the business environment. However, knowledge of these tools alone may not produce a true picture of business health. Descriptions and discussions of any qualitative or quantitative tool must not overshadow the fundamental concepts involved in applying the tools to business processes.

This book emphasizes a fundamental concept called **Statistical Thinking,** which is a crucial precursor to proper data gathering, analysis, and interpretation. The book is not a primer in statistics, but a primer in how to view, study, understand, and ultimately improve your business processes. As such, you need not be proficient in statistical tools or methodologies to use the book. All that's required is a willingness to think differently about your work processes and recognize the existence of variation all around you.

There are two basic objectives for the book: to introduce the concepts of Statistical Thinking, and to illustrate the application of these concepts through case studies that describe the use of Statistical Thinking in widely different settings at different organizational levels. Part I describes the need for Statistical Thinking. Part II follows with the definition of Statistical Thinking and its application to various levels of an organization. Part III discusses the application of Statistical Thinking using case studies to illustrate the applications and models for improvement. In Part IV, the focus changes to developing Statistical Thinking capability in others. Throughout the book, if you see a paragraph with a ᐅ or ♦, look for a nearby tip or pitfall.

In reading this book, you will benefit by:

- Understanding how variation affects processes
- Learning concepts for minimizing variation at all levels
- Using the case studies to reinforce the concepts
- Developing the expertise to mentor others in how to minimize process variation

The authors have written this book to be used as a:

- Reference for individual growth and learning
- Training text in business and industry, our primary audience
- Source for case studies which illustrate how to tie the individual tools together
- Companion to the GOAL/QPC's *The Memory Jogger II* and introductory statistics texts to form a more Statistical Thinking-oriented introductory course in academia. This book could provide the introduction and concepts, *The Memory Jogger II* the basic tools, and a formal text the more traditional analytic tools.

We hope you enjoy reading and learning the concepts described in this book. More importantly, we hope you are able to use these concepts in your job to lead your organization in its continuous improvement efforts.

The book concludes with some practice scenarios, suggestions for which are provided in the appendix.

Finally, the authors wish to thank the Statistics Division of the American Society for Quality for their support in the completion of this book, the first book in a new *Improving Performance* series being developed by the Statistics Division.

Galen C. Britz—Quality Manager, 3M

Donald W. Emerling—Vice President, Operations, Ryobi Die Casting (USA), Inc.

Lynne B. Hare—Director, Applied Statistics, Nabisco, Inc.

Roger W. Hoerl—Quality Leader, GE

Stuart J. Janis—Statistical Specialist, 3M

Janice E. Shade—Continuous Improvement Manager, Nabisco, Inc.

CONTENTS

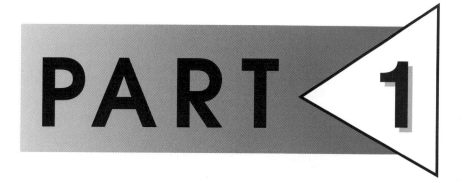

Why Is Statistical Thinking Important?

Introduction 1

The world continues to become increasingly complex and competitive. A major transition began in the early 1980s when global competition became an economic force. The change was driven by increasing customer demands for better products and more responsive services, and was made possible by advances in technology, transportation, and communication. This rapidly changing and highly competitive environment requires all organizations to find ways to improve if they want to survive. Survival is not easy. For example, the General Electric Company is the only surviving member of the original (1896) list of Dow Jones Industrial Average companies.

While the competition in business environments may be obvious, it is important to realize that the same competition is occurring in virtually all organizations, such as government, health care, education, and even religious organizations. State and local governments compete to have businesses locate within their jurisdictions and bring in new jobs and revenue. Healthcare networks compete for customers, especially for the large contracts from major businesses, government organizations, and educational institutions. Universities, and even high and elementary schools to some degree, compete to attract the most desirable students and teachers. Worshipers within any religious organization have choices also, and churches, synagogues, mosques, etc., that do not attract or retain members will not survive. Because of the competitive environment within which organizations find themselves, improvement is critical to survival and progress. Since typically the competition also is improving, it is often the *rate* of improvement that determines the winners and losers.

Note that the authors are not suggesting that life should be competitive, but are simply acknowledging that it is. We believe that internal cooperation is a prerequisite to external competition, that is, everyone on the team must cooperate to compete successfully with other organizations. Even in a cooperative, win-win environment, improvement is required for everyone to reap greater benefits.

One improvement initiative, which includes many Statistical Thinking concepts and tools, is the *Six Sigma* methodology. This approach was popularized by Motorola in the 1980s, and has subsequently been applied by Texas Instruments, Allied Signal, and General Electric (GE). Six Sigma uses a four-phase approach to overall improvement: measure, analyze, improve, and control. The Six Sigma approach utilizes key aspects of Statistical Thinking, such as identification of key business processes, understanding and reduction of variation, and the use of data for analysis and decision making. The financial results of Six Sigma have been impressive. For example, GE has reported documented savings of more than $2 billion from 1996–1998, based on an investment of approximately $1 billion over the same time period. The $2 billion figure includes internal cost savings only, and does not include increased sales resulting from enhanced customer satisfaction. Impressive financial results have also been reported by other companies seriously implementing Six Sigma. See Hahn et al (1998) for more details on this Statistical Thinking initiative.

Clearly then, for an organization to survive and prosper, steady improvement is critical. One must therefore learn how to improve. This topic is not often taught in school, not even in graduate education. Statistical Thinking is one approach that provides a theory and methodology to help us improve. Statistical Thinking helps identify where improvement is needed, provides the general approach to take, and even suggests the tools to use. Statistical Thinking also ensures that improvements are made to the entire system, not just to one part of it. In other words, it does not just shift the problem from "my" department to "yours." Instead, it eliminates the problem by viewing the process across all departments.

In the remainder of this book, we'll define Statistical Thinking and discuss its important components of process, variation, and data. We'll present case studies that demonstrate the benefits of Statistical Thinking, as well as some of the tools and methodologies that have proven useful in improving processes. We'll also introduce two basic improvement strategies: the *Process Improvement Strategy,* to be used for fundamental improvement of processes exhibiting relatively normal behavior; and the *Problem Solving Strategy,* which is effective at understanding and resolving abnormal process behavior. Finally, we'll provide tips on how to begin implementing Statistical Thinking concepts in an organization. The book concludes with practice scenarios, suggestions for which are provided in the appendix.

Before we jump into the definition of Statistical Thinking, though, let's illustrate how Statistical Thinking can help us improve with a brief but real example.

Case Study: Time's Running Out[1]

2

A large publications corporation, Kowalski and Sons (a fictitious name), is having trouble with their monthly billing process. They have discovered that it takes about 17 days to complete and mail invoices (bills), despite management's expectation that it should be done in less than 10 days. This target is important from both the company's point of view and that of the customer. Not only would a shorter billing cycle time improve the company's cash flow, it also would allow customers to enter billing information promptly into their accounting systems and close their monthly books sooner. The current situation also results in numerous "late" payments, for which Kowalski and customers often blame each other. Customers also complain that other publishers are not as tardy in sending out bills.

Does this sound bad? Actually, this is a very typical situation in business. In fact, when one of the authors consulted on this problem began to dig deeper, he learned the situation was worse than it initially appeared! Assessing the process revealed that three different departments were involved in completing and mailing bills. Each department or function worked separately. No one understood the process from end to end. When problems occurred, there was a lot of finger pointing—"The problem is not with us, it's with them. If they would clean up their act, the billing process would be OK." Similarly, there were no standard operating procedures, that is, formal, agreed upon methods of getting the job done. Everybody performed the job a different way. This resulted in considerable "fire fighting" to keep the bills going out.

Heroic efforts requiring long hours after work and shifting of priorities abounded.

The one clear advantage this situation had over other typical scenarios is that a quantitative measure existed to monitor the performance of the process—the number of days required to process the bills. Without a clear measure of success it is difficult, if not impossible, to effectively manage and improve a process.

Some business leaders faced with this situation would find someone to blame and reprimand. Such an approach assumes that the blame lies with individual people, and it does not suggest a means of improvement. To understand the scope and root causes of the problem, one must first view the billing cycle time as the output of a process that can be studied and improved. Once a process view is taken, it is easier to localize the problem, identify root causes, and make improvements. By understanding and improving the process, we improve the outputs, or results.

Data are typically required to identify and deal with the root causes of problems. Without data, everyone is an "expert," and as noted by Snee (1986), "discussions produce more heat than light." Without data, it is difficult to get agreement on the magnitude of the problem, root causes, and what, if any, progress has been made in resolving it. Data's constant companion is variation. If there were no variation, we never would need more than one data point! If the existence of variation is not recognized and understood, people tend to over-react to the last data point, without viewing it in context of historical data. The result is "fire fighting," process tampering, and micro-management. Unfortunately, most people are taught a deterministic view of the world, for example, the belief that financial results should always exactly equal budget, or in chemistry that a mass balance should always balance exactly. In reality, variation is always present, whether we like it or not.

The approach actually taken in this example, and the one that this book explains, is referred to as Statistical Thinking. It views the cycle time as the output of a process that could be studied and improved via analysis of appropriate data, and recognizes variation in both the process itself and in the data.

A team was organized to ensure that the whole system was improved, and to obtain various viewpoints on the problem. They created a systems map for the overall process, along with a flow-chart of critical process steps. The systems map identified the responsible organizations and what flowed back and forth between them. The flowchart became the foundation of a new production schedule for the monthly billing cycle. This schedule aligned the organization with regard to what had to be done each month by which group, and by when.

Next, the team identified critical sub-processes, and monitored cycle time measurements for each of them, as well as for the over-all process. These measurements enabled the identification of key problem areas. Cross-functional sub-teams provided daily trou-bleshooting and reviewed the performance of the billing process at the end of the cycle. These teams identified problems and proce-dures for creating and implementing solutions.

The team also initiated efforts to document the process. This helped reduce procedural variation (that is, people doing things dif-ferently) and was central to training new employees. A process owner was also assigned. His job was to care for the health of the process by seeing that the process management system was used and improved to handle the changing conditions the process would experience.

The use of this Statistical Thinking approach significantly improved the operations of the process. Over a 5-month period, the monthly billing cycle time was reduced from 17 days to about 9.5 days, with less variation. This resulted in annual savings of more than $2.5 million dollars, not to mention more satisfied cus-tomers and a less stressful working environment for the employees.

There are several key elements of success in this story:

- First, billing was recognized as a system of interconnected processes. Employees had only been interested in completing their *individual* tasks, without understanding their impact on the total process. Once the process approach was taken, the system map and flowchart provided a global view to all involved. The process perspective also was instrumental in recognizing the need for the cross-functional team that ultimately solved the problem.
- Second, the team recognized variation in the process. An obvious culprit was differences in how people performed

procedures. This wasn't the fault of any individual—the process had never been fully documented, making it virtually impossible to have standard methodology.

- Third, the team collected data in the form of cycle time measurements. These data permitted them to measure the process and its sub-processes. They also allowed the team to assess the situation at the start of the project and quantify the improvement.

The Statistical Thinking philosophy resulted in a substantial reduction in billing cycle time through the identification and correction of breakdowns in the billing process. With this in mind, let's move on to the definition of Statistical Thinking.

ENDNOTES

1. This case history comes from Hoerl and Snee (2000).

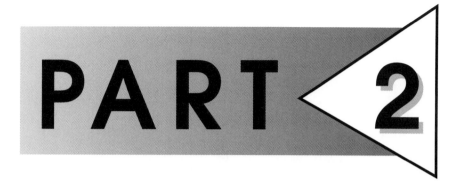

PART ▷ 2

WHAT IS STATISTICAL THINKING?

Statistical Thinking Defined

As discussed and demonstrated in Chapter 2, broad application of Statistical Thinking can help organizations respond to the competitive environment and the need to improve. Easy-to-use statistical software means that statistical approaches and tools are no longer restricted to technical specialists such as statisticians, computer scientists, or engineers. Everyone in the organization must have the capability to use the concepts and tools to improve their processes. This does not mean that everyone must know how to design experiments or run regression analyses, but everyone in the organization, from the CEO to the custodian, needs to understand and apply basic statistical concepts in their work. We call these basic statistical concepts Statistical Thinking.

Statistical Thinking combines key concepts from several improvement approaches popular in recent years, such as reengineering, total quality management (TQM), benchmarking, and systems thinking. These *key concepts* include:

- Improving the overall system instead of sub-optimizing its components.
- Viewing work as a process.
- Using data to guide decisions.
- Recognizing and responding wisely to variation.

The 1996 edition of the *Glossary and Tables for Statistical Quality Control,* published by Quality Press, includes the following definition:

Statistical Thinking is a philosophy of learning and action based on the following fundamental principles:

- *All work occurs in a system of interconnected processes,*
- *Variation exists in all processes, and*
- *Understanding and reducing variation are keys to success.*

Let's discuss each principle in greater detail.

STATISTICAL THINKING IS A PHILOSOPHY OF LEARNING AND ACTION

Fundamentally, Statistical Thinking is a philosophy of learning and action: **Learning** how to best acquire and interpret information, while responding to this information with the appropriate **action.**

When information is transmitted from one person to another, it is communicated based on past experiences and knowledge. Recipients hear and act on the information based on their own perceptions. Statistical Thinking promotes the evaluation of a process that is based on data instead of past experiences or perceptions. How many times have you heard:

- We've always done it this way!
- We work with what we get!
- We do the best we can!
- I never thought about it!
- I'm so busy with day-to-day troubles, I don't have time to try that!
- That has no effect on the finished product (or service)!

Attitudes inherent in these statements limit or prevent improvement. They reflect discomfort with change and a desire to maintain the status quo. People's perceptions and past experiences limit out-of-the-box thinking. Anyone who has spent time with 3-year-olds knows that "Why" is their favorite word. Yet, by the time we become adults, this word has vanished from our vocabulary. We readily accept problems in our work processes and are not proactive in finding out why. Statistical Thinking demands that we ask "Why?" For example:

- Why is the material from the fabrication department machine so inconsistent?
- Why do we constantly firefight?
- Why does our daily output vary so much?
- Why does every job result in a monumental task that takes forever to complete?

Questions like these are important in identifying and understanding variation in work. For example, Kowalski and Sons required 17 days to bill their customers. Despite everyone's best efforts, the process never performed well. The problems led to accusations and finger pointing. Nothing improved until someone asked "Why?" The true causes didn't emerge until the team learned about the process by documenting it and identifying the critical process steps. The result: The people performing the work weren't inadequate; the problem was with the process itself. With this knowledge, the team was able to take action to cut the cycle time nearly in half.

ALL WORK OCCURS IN A SYSTEM OF INTERCONNECTED PROCESSES

Statistical Thinking is a philosophy of learning and action that builds the foundation for successful decision making in any process. Here, the term process represents actions (manufacturing or non-manufacturing) that transform inputs into an output or end product. As shown in Figure 3.1, a process is comprised of five components, known by the acronym **SIPOC: Suppliers** provide **Inputs** to the process. The inputs are transformed by the **Process** into **Outputs** that go to **Customers.**

Since the ultimate goal of the process is to provide outputs to customers, it is crucial to completely understand what customers want and obtain feedback on how well we provide it. Throughout the process, external factors can add variation, resulting in less than optimal products or services or decreased efficiencies.

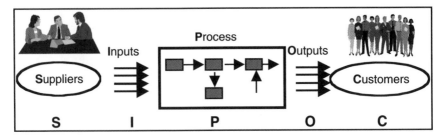

Figure 3.1 A Process Is Comprised of Five *Components—Suppliers* Provide *Inputs,* Which Are Transformed by the *Process* into *Outputs* That Go to *Customers.*[1]

Manufacturing processes involve the production of units for internal and/or external customers. Variation enters manufacturing processes via a multitude of interfaces such as people, machines, materials, methods, measurements, and the environment (both physical and organizational).

✎ Non-manufacturing processes, often referred to as business processes, are prevalent in organizations that provide services or support to customers. Unlike manufacturing processes, there is not always a discernible end product. In fact, work is often erroneously viewed as an event and not a process. People instead of machines dominate this process. As a result, variation enters when operating procedures are not standardized or the role of the individual or group is not aligned with the overall

---

✎ TIP

Always flowchart your process.

There may be no more important tip. By flowcharting the process you identify hand-offs between people and functions in the process, and you usually identify immediate opportunities for improvement.

objective of the service or support group, although computer systems and poorly designed forms can play a role, too.

♦※   Many processes contains multiple sub-processes as shown in Figure 3.2. The first sub-process transforms inputs from an external supplier and supplies the second sub-process. Correspondingly, the second sub-process is a customer of the first and a supplier to the third. This internal supplier-customer relationship between continues until a product or service is in its final form and is supplied to the external customer. These relationships will prove important when improving the process. Understanding the internal and external customers' needs will help define the appropriate data to identify and reduce variation.

It is also clear that work and life consist of many intertwined or interdependent processes operating in parallel, which together form a system. This last point has been emphasized as *systems thinking* by Senge (1990) and others. Organizations often fail when they try to optimize profit by optimizing each function independently, such as minimizing procurement costs, minimizing production costs, or maximizing sales. Why? Because minimizing procurement costs often increases manufacturing costs and decreases sales. In other words, the work system as a whole must be optimized due to the interdependencies and interactions of the sub-processes. No process functions in isolation, and improvement strategies must not be implemented without considering their effect on the entire process. Optimizing the individual functions without recognizing the impact on the system is called *sub-optimization.*

♦※ PITFALL

Internal customers: "Trust but verify"

When receiving the requirements and expectations of internal customers, make sure they are consistent with the requirements and expectations of a "real" customer.

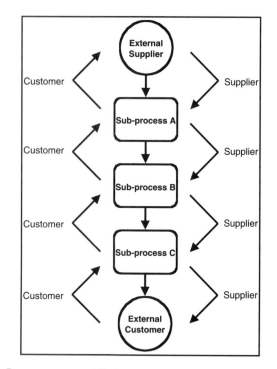

Figure 3.2 Processes and Subprocesses.

Statistical Thinking at Home

All work is not limited to employment, but includes working on your golf game, working in your garden, trying to lose weight, and developing interpersonal relationships. Such activities occur through processes that have inputs that are acted upon by the processes themselves to produce outputs.

For example, when two people enter into a marriage, their attitudes towards each other and beliefs about marriage are inputs that will significantly impact the life they will create together. These attitudes may have been formed early in life from experiences in their own families or from religious beliefs. These inputs typically impact the marriage gradually as the couple goes through life transitions, such as balancing careers and family responsibilities, adapting to children, mid-life crises, and so on. The degree of emotional intimacy in the marriage can increase or decrease depending on the couple's response to these process transformations. Outputs of the marriage, besides the obvious, can be positive, such as personal fulfillment, companionship, and friendship, or negative, such as spousal abuse and divorce.

In summary, Statistical Thinking requires that results are viewed in light of the process and process inputs which produced the results. It then becomes obvious that improving results requires improving the process and/or inputs.

VARIATION EXISTS IN ALL PROCESSES

Chapter 5 covers this all-important topic in detail. For now, suffice it to say that variation is all around us, from the number of widgets we manufacture in a production shift to the number of telephone calls received by a software help desk in a day. In our personal lives the time spent driving to work is different each day. We complain when the weather forecast is inaccurate and become frustrated when planes are late. Like it or not, variation is everywhere. *Helping people understand this fundamental principle and "unlearn" their deterministic view of the world is the greatest contribution the statistically literate, and only the statistically literate, can provide to society.*

Variation can enter a process through its inputs or the activities that transform those inputs into outputs. The variation can result in poorer quality to the customer or inefficient operation of the process, as in Kowalski & Sons' highly variable 17-day billing cycle.

Variation typically originates from one of six sources:

- *People*—through different ways of doing things, different learning styles, different skills and abilities
- *Machines*—through inconsistent equipment or from several pieces of equipment that don't perform identically (even though we think they should)

- *Materials*—because of multiple suppliers of supposedly identical inputs or variation from shipment to shipment with the same supplier
- *Methods*—through poorly written procedures or procedures that are not robust to other sources of variation
- *Measurement*—through inability to accurately and precisely measure process outputs
- *Environment*—both physical (temperature, humidity, etc.) and the workplace environment, such as policies, attitudes of management and co-workers, etc.

Variation and processes are also intertwined by complexity. When processes don't perform as planned (that is, they vary), additional steps frequently are added to compensate. These "just-in-case" steps make the process that much more difficult to operate, leaving open the door for additional variation. This seemingly never-ending cycle explains why process simplification is often a major contributor to improvement.

While identification and recognition of variation itself is an important concept, improvement comes about by our actions in the face of variation, which leads to the third element of the Statistical Thinking definition.

UNDERSTANDING AND REDUCING VARIATION ARE KEYS TO SUCCESS

Deming's fundamental principle of quality states that when variation is reduced, quality is improved. He once said, "If I had to reduce my message for management to just a few words, I'd say it all had to do with reducing variation." Deming (1982) used an experiment of dropping beads through a funnel to demonstrate process variation and to show just how easy it is for management to blame workers for problems over which they have no control.

Inappropriately reacting to variation can have severe consequences for the organization. Employees can become demoralized if they are asked to explain every downturn in sales or deviation from a forecast. This is equivalent to asking them to solve the same problem 100 times, when they would rather solve

100 problems once each. If management ranks employees, some-one will be ranked highest even if all employees performed iden-tically. This hurts teamwork since employees will compete instead of cooperating for the benefit of the organization.

Several of Deming's 14 points emphasize management's role in reducing variation. Workers performing the job on a daily basis have valuable ideas about how to reduce process variation. Management's responsibility includes ensuring the appropriate mechanisms are instituted to act upon these ideas, such as lis-tening to employee suggestions, comments, and complaints, and actively assisting employees in improving the systems in which they work.

What About Variety?

It should be noted that variety and controlled variation are sometimes appropriate and even desirable. Many businesses value diversity of thought and perspective; a diversity of thought among team members is important. New product development requires experimentation with new ideas and approaches. In our personal lives, very few people would want to eat the same meals every day (variety is the spice of life). Popping popcorn only works because there is variation in the time it takes each kernel to pop. If all the kernels popped at the same time, a virtual explosion would result! However, we want to *control* the variation so that each bag of popcorn takes the same amount of time to pop. Reducing variation in this situation involves keeping the *distribution* of popping times constant from bag to bag.

Traditionally, the statistical profession has emphasized model-ing and quantifying variation rather than reducing it. This passive approach does not directly lead to improvement and is counter to Deming's fundamental message. In most situations, reducing vari-ation is critical to success. Reduced product variation satisfies customers: Reduced process and input variation reduces product variation in manufacturing; in business, it typically reduces costs. In our personal lives, we generally want our favorite dish prepared just the way we like it; our planes, buses, and trains on time; and our relationships on an even keel.

In summary, Statistical Thinking is the manner in which information is viewed, processed and converted into action steps. It is a philosophy of thinking, not a recipe to perform mathematical calculations and statistically crunch data. Statistical Thinking emphasizes that all work consists of a series of interconnected processes that must be completed to achieve a desired goal. For success, each sub-process must be investigated to identify areas of opportunity and improvement that will benefit the entire system.

ENDNOTE

1.   The authors would like to thank Ron Snee for the use of this depiction of SIPOC.

Improvement Using Statistical Thinking ◁ 4

THE INTEGRATION OF STATISTICAL THINKING AND STATISTICAL METHODS

It should be obvious that improvement isn't only about statistical methods—the number crunching, distributions, control charting, and so on, that are near and dear to the hearts of statisticians. Improvement also includes *Statistical Thinking*—how the practitioner studies a system and its interconnected processes to identify improvement opportunities. While statistical methods have proven their worth over the years, they are much more effective when applied in an environment of Statistical Thinking.

Statistical Thinking and statistical methods are not competitors, but are rather very synergistic when properly integrated. Figure 4.1 illustrates the integration of *Statistical Thinking* and *Statistical Methods* into a philosophy of learning and action that results in improvement.

PHILOSOPHY, ANALYSIS, AND ACTION

Improvement starts with the **philosophy** and first principle of Statistical Thinking: *All work occurs in a system of interconnected processes.* The first step is to identify the process or processes involved in the activity and the inputs, activities, and outputs to study. Traditional statistical methods play little if any role at this point. However, the philosophy and process context set the stage to effectively use statistical methods.

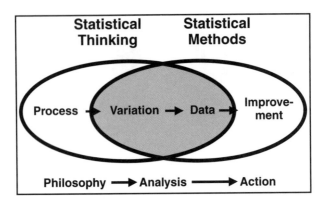

Figure 4.1 Improvement Using Statistical Thinking.

Process identification flows naturally into **analysis,** which combines the next two principles of Statistical Thinking: *Variation exists in all processes* and *Understanding and reducing variation are the keys to success.* The strong interaction and interdependence of Statistical Thinking and statistical methods is most evident here. Analytic tools of Statistical Thinking, such as affinity diagrams and interrelationship digraphs (see Chapter 13), identify key process performance metrics and critical needs of customers and suppliers. Then statistical methods and tools, such as run charts, scatter diagrams, control charts, experimental design, and many others become important in the analysis, identification, and quantification of the process variation and data flow.

As we move toward **action,** statistical methods become the more dominant focus. Action plans are developed to use the tools and methods of statistics to create rapid improvement, and those tools and methods continue to track performance.

Table 4.1 compares and contrasts Statistical Thinking with statistical methods. Statistical Thinking is basically conceptual, dealing with ideas and ways of thinking, while statistical methods are more technical, dealing with data and mathematics. Statistical Thinking can be applied anywhere, while the application of statistical methods is carefully targeted to high impact areas. To apply Statistical Thinking we must have knowledge, both of Statistical Thinking concepts and of the process we're trying to improve. Obviously, to apply statistical methods, data are

Table 4.1   Comparison of Statistical Thinking
and Statistical Methods

	Statistical Thinking	Statistical Methods
Overall Approach	Conceptual	Technical
Desired Application	Universal	Targeted
Primary Requirement	Knowledge	Data
Logical Sequence	Leads	Reinforces

needed. It is noteworthy that while we generally have data when applying Statistical Thinking, it is not an absolute requirement. For example, a company may choose to reduce its supplier base to shrink raw material variation, or utilize a variety of teaching methods to account for personal differences (variation) in learning styles, even in the absence of hard data.

Since Statistical Thinking is primarily conceptual and universally applicable, it should be applied first, that is, it should lead. Statistical methods reinforce Statistical Thinking by providing process improvement as a focus for data collection and analysis.

PROCESS, VARIATION, AND DATA

Statistical Thinking provides a framework, recognizing all work as a **process** to study and improve. This does not require statistical techniques, but is critically important for effective application of Statistical Thinking. The process perspective creates awareness of **variation** and its impact, as when Kowalski & Sons noticed that some bills take longer to prepare than others. Statistical methods take on a more prominent role as **data** are needed to quantify the variation and provide direction on how to reduce it, resulting in process improvement.

Each component of Statistical Thinking is necessary for a complete improvement approach. For example, without a process view, it is often difficult to define the scope of the problem. Issues seem to appear from nowhere, and root causes are hard to find. Turf battles erupt—"The problem is with them, we're OK." The typical response is to blame the people involved, even if the real problem lies with the system. Poorly performing sports teams usually fire the coach, even if the real problem lies with the team's general management or policies dictated by the owners. Of course, the net result of these actions is to hinder process management and stifle improvement.

Without understanding variation, managers tend to manage by the last data point. If the last data point was good, everyone gets a pat on the back. If the last data point was bad, everybody gets a kick in the rear. These knee-jerk reactions ripple through the organization, resulting in fire fighting with little coordination of effort. Often, common cause issues are treated as special causes, producing tampering and micro-management (see Chapter 5). Managers continue these same superstitious behaviors month after month with no real improvement, but they rarely catch on that the whole exercise is meaningless. Again, the net result is hindered process management, and stifled improvement.

Without data, everyone is an expert; team discussions tend to produce more heat (anger) than light (insight and learning). Of course, with no historical data, peoples' memories are poor, and often in conflict with one another. The team can't get agreement on the extent of the problem, what progress has been made, or what they are really trying to accomplish. Decisions tend to be made on the basis of political power rather than knowledge. These actions also hinder process management and stifle improvement.

Statistical Thinking provides a more holistic approach to improvement that includes each of these major elements, process, variation, and data.

To conclude, improvement using Statistical Thinking is the integration of two components—Statistical Thinking and statistical methods. Together they form a powerful philosophy of learning and action, leading to rapid performance improvement. This approach is illustrated in the following comment from author Lynne Hare:

The use of statistical tools is greater and of higher quality in a Statistical Thinking environment. Statistical Thinking provides an environment for statistical tools. Back in the dark ages, in the early stages of my career, I became frustrated with the lack of use of sta-

tistical tools. While seeking root causes, I learned that managers would not allow workers to use tools that they (the managers) did not understand. For managers to acquire understanding, they had to see the advantage. That, in turn, required understanding of variation and the process view. It took a long time, but I was able to change organizational culture to one in which there was a better understanding of the process view and the accompanying variation whose understanding affords an opportunity for improvement. Only then was I successful at getting increased use of statistical tools— simple tools at first and, with increased understanding, more advanced tools.

More About Variation and Data   5

Variation is central to Statistical Thinking, and it has many aspects worth considering. Its four primary manifestations are:

- Off-target
- Common cause
- Special cause
- Structural

Numerically, the first relates to the process average, while the last three affect the traditional standard deviation. Business processes typically attract attention by being off-target, even if problems with other types of variation have persisted for years. Common cause variation is present in all processes. The other manifestations dominate some processes and are absent from others. Walter Shewhart (1931) developed the control chart in the 1920s to distinguish between common and special cause variation (although he called the latter "assignable cause.")

When customers experience undesirable variation, they generally don't care what kind it is. The distinction is important because the improvement strategies depend on the type of variation. The following case study examines all four types.

CASE STUDY: YOU WANT IT WHEN?!?[1]

Shawn shook her head as she looked at the latest weekly numbers for on-time delivery at her distribution center, one of several in her company. The corporation had a goal to deliver 97.5 percent of

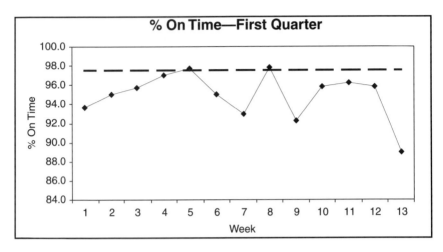

Figure 5.1   Percent of On-Time Delivery During the First Quarter.

orders on time and during the first quarter, she had met the goal only twice. She reviewed those two weeks to see what her team had done right, but couldn't find anything unusual.

Shawn's data are plotted in Figure 5.1. Two manifestations of variation are present. First, the process is **off-target.** In other words, its average of 94 percent does not meet its target—the corporate goal of 97.5 percent. Second, Shawn's process is dominated by **common cause** variation, the regular daily and weekly variation in process inputs (number and complexity of orders, truck schedules, personnel availability, etc.), that combine to prevent each week's on-time delivery numbers from being identical. As a result, it is impossible to predict results in any given future week. However, she could, with the aid of the control chart in Figure 5.2, determine that while her average is about 94 percent, no week should fall below 88 percent unless there was an unusual event.

✎   Isolating the two weeks that met the goal would not prove very helpful for process improvement. They are the result of the same process (and same inputs that vary) that produced all the other weeks and don't contribute much information in isolation. On the other hand, looking at all the weeks, good and bad, could be useful in identifying which factors have the greatest influence in on-time delivery.

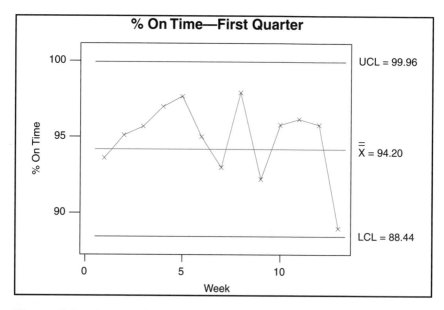

Figure 5.2 Control Chart of Percent On Time.

✎ TIP

If a process or system is stable—showing only common causes of variation.

Use the tools of improvement to study all the data (not just the "good" or the "bad" points) and identify factors that cause variation. Determine what needs to be permanently changed to achieve a different level of quality.

Common cause variation is native to every process. Manufacturing processes experience it from changes in raw material, equipment and controller settings, testing, and how people perform procedures, even though the basic process doesn't change. Mature product sales experience common cause variation from fluctuations in the economy, use rates by customers, and variation in

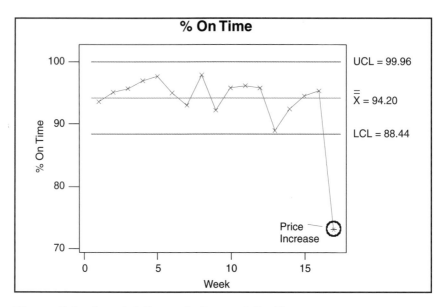

Figure 5.3 Special Cause in Percent On Time.

demand of the customers' customers, even though the basic sales process doesn't change. Common cause variation cannot be eliminated unless the inherent nature of the process is changed.

When Shawn realized that she needed system changes to meet her goal of 97.5 percent, she created a process improvement team to work on the problem. However, while they were in the early stages of studying the process, the distribution center experienced a truly horrendous week. Only 73 percent of the deliveries reached customers on time. This was far less than the 88 percent worst case she could expect from her process. It was clear that something had changed.

Investigation showed that a division that supplied the distribution center had announced an impending price increase to its customers, causing a large increase in volume during that week. The distribution center was not prepared to handle the extra work and fell behind on orders as a result.

✎   This is an example of a **special cause** and is depicted in Figure 5.3. Special causes are external factors, not part of the normal process, that introduce variation into the system. In Shawn's case, the special cause affected a single time period. Some special causes have a more permanent impact on the process, causing the average to move to and stay at a new level.

✍ TIP

If a process or system is not stable—showing signs of special cause.

Use the tools of problem solving to identify the root cause. Try to identify exactly when, where, how, and why the process changed.

If a special cause hurts the process, develop procedures to eliminate the return of the problem. If a special cause is beneficial, develop procedures to make it a permanent part of the process.

Special causes can be caused in manufacturing by factors such as equipment breakdowns, new shipments of raw materials, or a change in operator. Special causes in sales processes could come from the introduction of a new competitive product, or the acquisition of a large new customer.

Calculating statistics in the presence of special causes can be very misleading. Skip ahead for a moment to Figure 6.5 on page 53, a control chart of customer complaints. What meaning does the average of all the data have? Probably not much. As noted by Bill Tucker, a co-worker of one of the authors: "It's important to know how to average, but it's more important to know when not to!"

A final note: A special cause means only that the output was produced by a different process. It does not necessarily mean that the change was bad. Special causes can also change processes for the better. Ignoring these means lost opportunities.

As the team continued its study of the process, they developed plans for improvement. They noticed that when volume exceeded a certain level, they were more likely to miss deliveries. When too many people took vacation, the on-time percent dropped. Shawn and the team developed new policies to ensure sufficient numbers of people were available to fill orders. In addition, they discovered they could anticipate by Wednesday whether the volume would be too high by the end of the week. As a result they instituted an automatic overtime policy if heavy volume was expected.

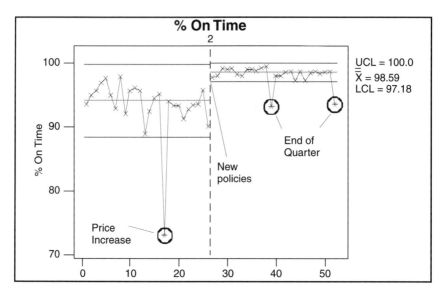

Figure 5.4 Structural Variation.

The new policies were put in place in the third quarter, and the results were dramatic. The percent on time rose to 98.5 percent and the lower common cause limit was about 97 percent. There were two points however, weeks 39 and 52, that stood out as special causes in the new system. These weeks were the end-of-quarter weeks, where the volume rose so high that not even the new policies could keep up with it.

Weeks 39 and 52, as seen in Figure 5.4, are examples of **structural variation**. Structural variation is a blend of common and special cause in that it is inherent variation that looks like a special cause when plotted. End-of-quarter volume increases are a real part of the current process, as are common causes. They stand out on the chart, though, as being very different, similar to special causes, and their onset is very predictable.

Types of Variation

A process is *off-target* if its average is not at the desired level.

Common cause variation is the variation a process would exhibit if it was behaving at its absolute best.

Special cause variation results from the intervention of sources external to the process.

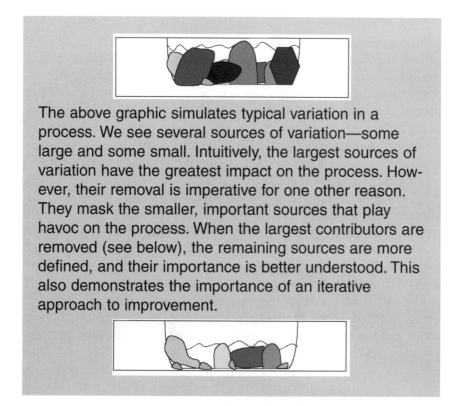

The above graphic simulates typical variation in a process. We see several sources of variation—some large and some small. Intuitively, the largest sources of variation have the greatest impact on the process. However, their removal is imperative for one other reason. They mask the smaller, important sources that play havoc on the process. When the largest contributors are removed (see below), the remaining sources are more defined, and their importance is better understood. This also demonstrates the importance of an iterative approach to improvement.

Figure 5.5 As Larger Sources of Variation Are Removed, Smaller Previously Covered Sources of Variation Surface.

Structural variation is variation which is inherent in the process (like common cause variation), appears to be special cause when plotted on a control chart, but has a predictable onset.

In Shawn's case, the structure was always there. However, the common cause variation had been so large that it masked the structure. This phenomenon is illustrated in Figure 5.5.

It is always a good idea to plot data more than one way, and Shawn's team found another kind of structure when they plotted daily volume. Volume was substantially higher on Tuesdays and

Fridays. Other examples of structure include steadily increasing profits or seasonal patterns in sales data, say for ski equipment or bathing suits. In these cases, the structure occurs across time periods. Structure also can occur within a time period, such as consistent differences between cavities in an injection molder or consistent differences between sales branches. The improvement approach for structural variation is similar to reduction of common cause variation in that it requires fundamental process change to reduce it or special treatment to incorporate the structure in the limits on a control chart.

Clearly, there is some gray area—events that could be considered special, common, or structural depending on the application. For example, most people would view an accident that snarled traffic as a special cause in the process of driving to work. However, if congestion and road rage increase to the degree that accidents become an everyday occurrence, they would turn into part of the common cause system. If the accidents tend to occur on Fridays when people are trying to leave town in a hurry, they could be considered structural variation.

IMPROVEMENT STRATEGIES FOR COMMON AND SPECIAL CAUSES

It is vitally important to understand the type of variation we're dealing with when we want to improve. Applying a special cause improvement strategy to a common cause situation and vice versa almost always makes things worse.

The primary focus for **improving a common cause system** is to look at *all* the data. There is a natural tendency to focus only on the data that meet (or fail to meet) a goal. This is generally not a good idea, because the goal rarely has any relation to the process. Shawn's goal was 97.5 percent, and her first instinct was to look at the two points that met it. Suppose the goal had been 96.5 percent. Should that change which data she studies? It shouldn't—all were produced by the same process, and the process didn't know the goal!

Joiner (1994) lists three strategies for improving common cause systems:

- Stratify
- Disaggregate
- Experiment

Stratification involves aggregating the data, then breaking it into categories and applying the Pareto principle to isolate a root cause. The distribution center team could have aggregated their data and stratified by day of the week, by trucking company, by supplier division, or by customer to see if most late deliveries were associated with a specific day, company, division, or customer. This strategy narrows the focus of the problem and can lead to faster improvement.

Disaggregation is useful when a process can be measured at several steps, because it involves breaking the process into its component parts, that is, studying subprocesses or process steps. The distribution center team could have broken the delivery process into receiving, packing, loading, and delivering the order, then identified potential bottlenecks or constraints by measuring the time required (or variation in time required) to complete each step.

Experimentation with potential solutions is the most direct approach. It is best if the solutions are based on data and piloted on a smaller scale.

Ultimately, all three strategies are designed to improve the system. The first two bring focus to which areas need improvement, while the third lets us propose and evaluate potential solutions.

The primary focus for **improving with special causes** is to isolate the problem. Collect data as soon as possible (before memories fade) to localize the situation to a specific process input or output. With special causes, we generally don't want to look at the entire set of data, because the variation is associated with a specific event.

What happens when common cause variation is treated with a special cause strategy (known as **tampering**)? A classic example is the monthly report with tables of numbers comparing this month to last month. The numbers have no historical context, so it is impossible to tell whether they're different because of a special cause or common causes. If the process is common cause, answering the question, Why is this month worse than (better than) last month? is an exercise in futility. The answers will generally be the same from month to month, yet people are forced to waste time answering the same questions over and over again.

Another example of tampering occurs in manufacturing when a stable, on-target process cannot consistently meet specifications. Wheeler and Chambers (1982) call this the "Threshold State." Adjusting a well-centered process when an individual sample falls out of specification will only move the process away from its target, resulting in increased variation.

Treating special cause variation as though it is common cause hinders process improvement, too, because opportunities to learn about the process are ignored. It can also cause frustration and low morale if system changes are instituted that impact people who aren't responsible for the problem. An example of this occurs when a company responds to an isolated incident by creating a policy that adds complexity to many people's jobs.

VARIATION AND TARGETS

While reducing variation is important, it is also important to give customers what they need. A product or service from a process with low variation still has no value if it does not work or perform as promised. A good process is centered at the proper target *and* has minimum variation around that target.

The idea of targets and minimum variation dates back at least to Gauss, although the concept was more recently popularized in manufacturing by Taguchi in the 1960s. The target philosophy says that customers prefer identical product at a target chosen where the product works best for them. The closer an item is to the target, the better it is in the eyes of the customer. As items move away from the target, they will cause greater economic loss for customers. The loss can come in the form of increased variation in the customers' products, increased costs due to longer machine setups, extra adjustments to their equipment, and other changes they must make to compensate for variability in their incoming material.

Figure 5.6 demonstrates the difference between the target philosophy and a traditional specification mentality, where all

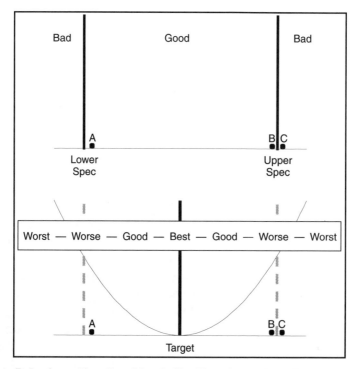

Figure 5.6 Specification Mentality (Top Graph) vs. Target Philosophy (Bottom Graph).

product is considered equally good if it falls within specifications. Under the specification mentality (the upper graph), products produced at points A and B are considered identical, while products produced at point B and C are considered different.

The bottom graph presents a more realistic picture. The vertical axis on the bottom graph represents the loss. When the process is centered at the target, there is minimum loss. As it moves away from the target, the loss increases, gradually at first but rising faster as we deviate further from the target value. Products produced at points A and B are recognized as different from each other under this model, and products produced at points B and C are essentially the same.

While specifications define limits for where products function acceptably, the target defines the point where the product works best. In a sense, the target philosophy asks the question, What is the best we can do? while the specification mentality asks, What is the worst we can get away with?

There are situations where a target is harder to conceptualize. For example, we usually want to reduce costs—the lower the better! Nevertheless, a business would be considerably easier to manage if costs were consistent and predictable than if they fluctuated wildly.

Many people view target and specification discussions in a strictly manufacturing environment, but the concepts apply in other areas of business, too. Some examples include sales forecasting, where the target is $0 difference from actual sales; airplane departure, with a target of on-time (not early or late) and a specification of no more than 15 minutes late; and cooking a medium steak, the target being a certain shade of pink in the middle. Joiner (1994) described a company with a human resources policy that reads, "Every employee will be treated with dignity, trust, and respect." Instead of creating a long list of rules (specifications) detailing what people could not do, they opted to state their target. When questionable behavior (variation) occurs they can ask, Did this bring us closer to the target or move us further away?

LESS TRADITIONAL VARIATION

Much of the discussion in this chapter has focused on numerical variation—numbers that can be expressed as a statistician's standard deviation or deviation from target. Variation can also take the form of differences in procedures, interpretations, opinions, and actions—also known as *human variation*, Balestracci (1998). Human variation can sometimes be the greatest cause of numerical variation. It is vitally important that it not be overlooked during improvement efforts.

THE ROLE OF DATA

Without variation, statistical methods would be irrelevant and decisions could be made using only one data point. Decision making becomes more challenging once variation enters the picture. When we get a data point, is it representative? It will almost certainly be different than the previous data point. Are the numbers different because of common cause variation or was there a special cause? Too many times, decisions are based strictly on anecdotes or perceptions—often the boss's—which may or may not have anything to do with the real situation. Organizations that practice Statistical Thinking value and use data to drive important decisions.

💣 Most people associate data with numbers, and much of the data we see takes that form. Temperatures, times to accomplish a task, sales, R&D costs, computer response times, and so forth, are all examples of numerical or quantitative data. However, quantitative data are not mandatory. In many business processes, qualitative data, such as measurement of customer opinions and suggestions, are equally effective. Regardless of whether the data are quantitative or qualitative, the concepts of variation—both common and special cause—are still valid and useful in understanding the process that produced the data.

💣 PITFALL

Valuing only quantitative data.

Data do not have to be quantitative. Qualitative data are just as important. For example, a team may generate numerous ideas for improvement, which will need to be analyzed.

While we use statistical methods to analyze data, the best analysis of a faulty data set is still a poor analysis. Understanding where the data came from and how they were collected provides valuable insight into analyses. Balestracci (1998) lists five elements to consider when collecting and analyzing data (see Figure 5.7).

The human variation of page 40 can play a major role in data collection. Examples include the number of decimal places recorded, different people's opinions of whether something is

---

Data Inventory Considerations

1. What is the **objective** of these data?

2. Is there an unambiguous **operational definition** to obtain a consistent value for the process being measured? Is it appropriate for the objective?

3. How are these data **accumulated/collected?** Is the collection appropriate for the objective?

4. How are the data currently being **analyzed/displayed?** Is the analysis/display appropriate, given the way the data were collected?

5. What **action,** if any, is currently being taken with these data? Given the objective and action, is anything "wrong" with the current number?

Figure 5.7 Data Inventory Considerations.

good or bad, sampling strategies if the data are collected by more than one person.

Many human variation issues in data collection can be overcome with clear objectives and well-communicated plans. When operational definitions are unclear (does everyone agree on the definition of a small blue car?), pilot studies can be useful. The people collecting and recording the data can compare notes after completing the pilot and improve the results of their final data collection.

Different situations require different kinds of data. Data used to monitor a process may be completely inappropriate for diagnosing it. Some people track gas mileage of their cars. This is a fine strategy for monitoring their cars' performance. However, other data are required to improve the performance. Examples of diagnostic data might include driving habits, outdoor temperature, or driving conditions, as well as internal measurements of the engine.

SAMPLE SIZE AND STRATEGY

Subject matter knowledge plays a crucial role in data collection. Many practical issues must be addressed, such as the typical inability to sample truly randomly, bias introduced by non-response, or erroneous data. When manufacturing steel, paper, or film, data are generally taken from the end of a long roll, rather than randomly throughout. We rely on process knowledge to infer behavior elsewhere in the roll. Subject matter knowledge helps marketers choose which market segments to study. In surveys, non-response bias may occur when selected individuals refuse to complete a survey form or be interviewed. Subject matter knowledge helps us determine ahead of time where these issues are likely to occur, and avoid or minimize them.

In general, enough data must be collected at the appropriate frequency to properly measure process variation. The frequency of sampling depends on the process. A manufacturing run lasting 20 minutes would be sampled more frequently than a 7-day run. Many managerial processes can be reported daily, weekly, monthly, quarterly, or annually. A primary factor in determining the frequency is the objective of the data collection. If the data are used to monitor the process, we should consider how quickly we can react to the data. If the data are intended to help us understand root causes of variation, we may want to collect more data at a higher frequency than usual.

The number of samples and their allocation also depend on how variation is distributed in the process. To understand the total process variation, it is important to sample many time periods if most of the variation is expected to occur over a longer period of time. If short-term variation is inconsistent, it is important to sample more often in a short period.

As far as how much data to take, while obtaining exact sample sizes to achieve specific technical objectives is a complex topic, there are some simple, broadly applicable rules of thumb:

- To get a reasonable estimate of the average, you need about 10 data points.
- To get a reasonable estimate of the standard deviation, you need about 30 data points.
- To get a reasonable estimate of the proportion defective (attribute data), you need about 100 data points.

Keep in mind that these are rules of thumb, and not scientifically rigorous! Also remember that getting the right data in an unbiased manner is typically a much greater challenge that getting the right sample size!

Putting it all together, variation and data go hand-in-hand to help us understand processes. Process variation assumes a variety of forms. All processes contain common cause variation. Some also contain special cause variation or predictable structural variation. In addition, a process can be off-target, where its average is different from a desired target or goal.

Understanding the difference between different types of variation is important because the type of variation drives the improvement strategy. If the process is dominated by common causes, it is important to look at all the data and make a change to the system. Stratification or disaggregation can help focus in on the most likely sources, and experimentation can help evaluate solutions. Special causes require a focus on a specific time period to understand what was different. Structural causes and off-target processes should be addressed through system changes. Human causes of variation should not be forgotten when searching for causes.

We use data to study variation. When collecting data, it is important to have a clearly-defined objective, operational definitions, and a collection plan that incorporates subject matter knowledge to determine sample size and strategy. While numerical data are useful, non-numeric data, such as thoughts or ideas, can also provide valuable information that leads to improved process understanding.

ENDNOTE

1. This case history is courtesy of Stu Janis.

Statistical Thinking at Various Organizational Levels   6

The uniqueness of Statistical Thinking is that it consists of *thought processes,* rather than numerical techniques. These thought processes affect how we receive, process, and react to information. Specifically, they enable us to view work within the context of the processes in which it occurs, grasp the significance of variation, and value taking the time to understand and reduce variation.

Statistical Thinking takes on different appearances when applied at different organizational levels due to the fundamentally different nature of the work at each level. At the **strategic** level, the overall purpose and long-term direction of the organization are developed, while at the **managerial** (tactical) level, processes align operational activity with the strategic direction. At the **operational** level, the focus is on performing the routine, day-to-day work of the organization, whether it is building computers, writing advertising campaigns, or performing surgery (see Figure 6.1).

STRATEGIC LEVEL

At the strategic level, the focus of Statistical Thinking is on the long-term concepts that guide organizational activities, such as those listed in Figure 6.2. The direction and strategy (long-term planning) of the organization incorporates process thinking and variation. Good leaders at this level stay focused on the organization's long-term future, the major steps required to get there, and how to adjust to changes in the external environment, and they resist the temptation to personally oversee routine daily activities.

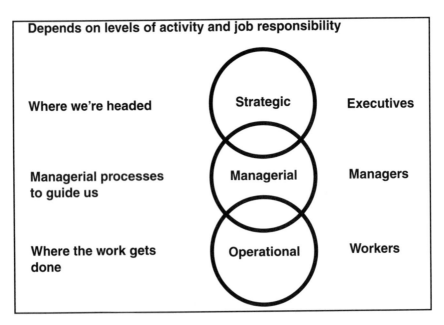

Depends on levels of activity and job responsibility

Where we're headed   Strategic   Executives

Managerial processes   Managerial   Managers
to guide us

Where the work gets   Operational   Workers
done

Figure 6.1   Statistical Thinking and Organizational Levels.

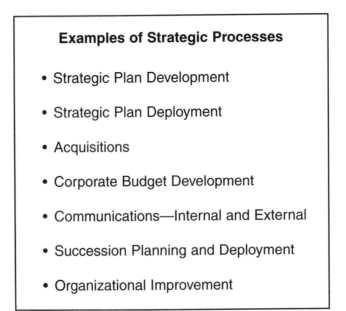

Examples of Strategic Processes

• Strategic Plan Development

• Strategic Plan Deployment

• Acquisitions

• Corporate Budget Development

• Communications—Internal and External

• Succession Planning and Deployment

• Organizational Improvement

Figure 6.2   Strategic Processes.

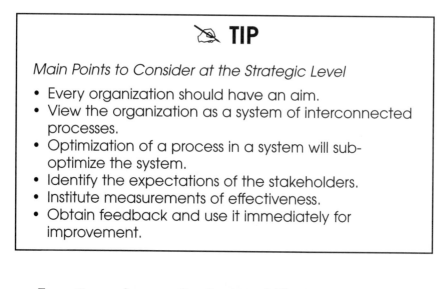

✎ **TIP**

Main Points to Consider at the Strategic Level

- Every organization should have an aim.
- View the organization as a system of interconnected processes.
- Optimization of a process in a system will sub-optimize the system.
- Identify the expectations of the stakeholders.
- Institute measurements of effectiveness.
- Obtain feedback and use it immediately for improvement.

Executives who practice Statistical Thinking recognize that variation is reduced when all processes and employees are focused on the same organizational aim. To promote this, they explicitly communicate the aim; flowchart the core processes most vital to the business; and plan and communicate their strategy throughout the organization.

Data-based decision making is the norm, and measurement systems assess progress from a common and special cause perspective. Data from sources such as competitors, regulators, marketing, sales, and customers, are also part of the assessment process.

All employees are encouraged to think "out-of-the-box" and experiment to find more efficient and effective ways of doing things. At the same time, the ramifications of changes are evaluated on the entire process to ensure that the benefit to one sub-process does not cannibalize another sub-process further down the line.

Statistical Thinking at the strategic level has the greatest impact on the organization. Decisions at this level affect managerial actions, which in turn influence operational efforts. An example of such an application occurred in Hutchinson, MN. The city adopted Statistical Thinking principles to reduce bureaucracy and waste. Let's explore how this was accomplished.

CASE STUDY: EXCELLENCE PLUS[1]

Hutchinson, MN, population 12,000, is located approximately 65 miles west of Minneapolis, and prides itself as home to a number of high-tech companies, Hutchinson Technical College, and many other local industries and businesses. Excellence Plus is Hutchinson city government's operational plan that focuses on continuous quality improvement. Excellence Plus is defined by the following five tenets:

1. *Recognize that all work is a process, and all processes have variation.*

2. *Continuous improvement will become a way of life.*

3. *Perform beyond expectations; anticipate unarticulated needs; delight the customer.*

4. *Follow a systematic approach of assembling teams, formalizing a planning process, training team leaders and facilitators, involving citizens, and measuring performance.*

5. *Stay on a never-ending journey to position Hutchinson as the global leader in community quality improvement.*

One of the most visible success stories is the building/ planning/zoning department's "One Stop Shop" concept. The idea originated in response to surveys that revealed a need to better coordinate various city departments so that developers and contractors could go to one place for all application information and permitting. The city administrator states, "After flowcharting the current process, identifying improvement opportunities and ways to implement those improvements, the end result was a value-added concept for permit applicants." The One Stop Shop Team consolidated forms between the utilities, the building department and outside contractors (telephone, cable, etc.); formalized communication links; and developed standardized checklists.

Another early success occurred in the Hutchinson Community Development Corporation office, where the commercial loan application process was greatly simplified and shortened (30 forms were reduced to just 8). A user-friendly checklist was created that informs developers of their commercial credit eligibility within 15 minutes—a dramatic reduction from the previous 1½ month process.

The recently completed Hutchinson Areas Transportation Ser-vices (HATS) facility is a good example of inter-departmental (cross-functional) cooperation. Three government entities (the State of Minnesota, McLeod County, and the City of Hutchinson) each were planning to build garages for road maintenance vehicles. Hutchinson city staff met with representatives of the other two gov-ernment bodies to design a value-added approach that would meet the needs of all three at a savings to taxpayers. Today, a model facility serves all three organizations, union and non-union alike, sharing common facilities, equipment, supplies, and resources.

Excellence Plus represents many processes and systems the City of Hutchinson will use to reach its vision, including a formalized plan-ning process, continuous improvement teams, citizen involvement, human resource development, and a process improvement council (steering team). Still in its infancy, Excellence Plus is about develop-ing techniques to support the continuous improvement process; mea-surements to drive desired behaviors and recognize the difference between common and special causes of variation; the planning, col-lection, and interpretation of customer response data; and focus on both internal and external customers.

The Hutchinson community has grown 25 percent during the last four years, yet city government, as measured by the number of employee hours, has increased just 8 percent—a testimonial to the benefits of streamlined work processes and customer focus.

Statistical Thinking at the strategic level resulted in innova-tive solutions to several city problems. The One Stop Shop and commercial loan application stories are classic examples of rec-ognizing work as a system of interconnected processes. In both cases, teams took a customer-focused viewpoint and simplified processes. In the HATS facility example, the three governments identified needs, while disregarding boundaries which normally divide governments. In each case, operational expenses decreased, yet delivery to the customer improved.

The variation and data aspects of Statistical Thinking also enter into these stories. From a customer perspective, learning of loan eligibility in 15 minutes is much closer to a (probably unstated) target than the six weeks required before the improvements, and the One Stop Shop project began with data from customers.

MANAGERIAL LEVEL

The managerial level is accountable for instituting the tactics—the systems and structure (organizational structure, hiring systems, reward and recognition systems, planning systems, and so on) to ensure that day-to-day activities are aligned with the strategic direction. Some of these processes are listed in Figure 6.3.

In a mom-and-pop business, the people who set long-term direction also perform the routine work of the organization. They can ensure that operational activities move towards the strategic direction. In large organizations, however, the people actually

---

Examples of Managerial Processes

- Employee Selection

- Training and Development

- Performance Management (including coaching)

- Recognition and Reward

- Budgeting

- Setting Objectives and Goals

- Project Management

- Communications

- Management Reporting

- Planning

Figure 6.3 Managerial Processes.

doing the work are often significantly removed from the strategic leadership, both physically and conceptually. The natural result is that well-meaning workers may actually move the organization away from its long-term direction. For example, strategic leadership of a company may have decided to focus on developing products that can be commercialized in five years, while researchers continue to focus on pure science.

  ✍ Managers who use Statistical Thinking incorporate process thinking by maintaining a customer focus for their organizations and basing decisions regarding new processes or process improvements on customer-generated data. Project reviews include results *and* the process used to obtain them. The managers consider process variation when setting goals, and view the measurement system itself as a process. Good meeting-management principles reduce the variability of meeting output.

✍ TIP

Main Points to Consider at the Managerial Level

- Use the CAP-Do variant of PDCA to diagnose the situation (see page 73).
- Plot all the data and look at it over time.
- Use Statistical Thinking to react properly to the data. Avoid tampering.
- Obtain customer feedback.
- Train everyone in the new way of thinking.

  Data are an important part of decisions and employees are trained in a variety of data-based decision techniques, aided by well-researched computer systems. Finally, a variety of communication methods help assure that all are informed and involved.

  At the managerial level, the absence of Statistical Thinking creates the greatest potential for breakdown, turf wars, and finger-pointing. Root causes often are overlooked or ignored because of the sensitivity of identifying inefficiencies in a particular functional area. If managers fear for their jobs, more energy will be spent hiding inappropriate policies and procedures than identifying and correcting the problems which hinder the overall process. This is not necessary. The following case study discusses the importance of working together to achieve a common understanding of the major issue and the action required to improve the process.

CASE STUDY: STATISTICAL THINKING AND CUSTOMER COMPLAINTS[2]

Managers of a company realized they needed to become more responsive to their customers. Customer complaints typically resulted in searches for superficial causes. When corrective action was taken, it focused on solving the individual problem but rarely altered the process to prevent future problems. "Quality improvement" generally consisted of corrective-action steps that did not improve overall quality, and thus could not be used to improve future products.

After receiving training in Statistical Thinking, the company took a new approach. People began to focus on the processes used to deliver products and services to their customers, identifying measures, gathering data, and improving those processes.

One team focused on the customer-complaint handling process. After studying flowcharts and talking to customers, the team proposed a different way of dealing with complaints. Instead of automatically treating complaints as isolated events, the team evaluated each complaint to determine if it really was an isolated event (special cause), or if it was generated from a process needing improvement (common cause).

Under the old system customers asked for written documentation of corrective action with every problem. The new proposal included ongoing evaluation of the complaint data. In addition to complaints, the company asked customers to supply actual product usage data, so that defect rates could be calculated and control charted. This was difficult for the customers to accept at first, but after receiving their own education in Statistical Thinking they

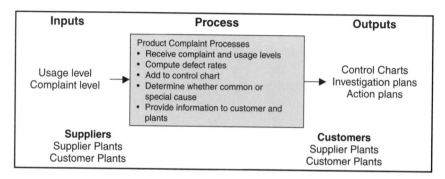

Figure 6.4   Flowchart of New Product Complaint System.

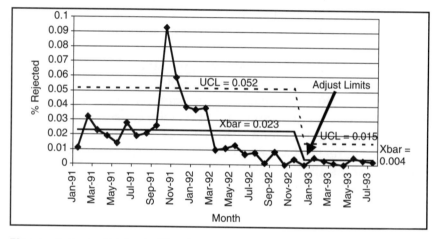

Figure 6.5   Individuals Chart.

agreed to the new way of handling complaints. A flowchart of the new complaint process is shown in Figure 6.4.

Now a customer/company team reviews the complaint control charts on a monthly basis. If a special cause occurs, the company is expected to develop a corrective action plan to identify the cause and take appropriate action. If the process is operating at an unacceptable level of complaints, the team decides if action to improve the process is necessary, prioritizing this improvement project along with all other currently active joint projects.

The control chart in Figure 6.5 illustrates how the new complaint process helped improve quality. The 0.023 percent reject *level (the performance level prior to September 1991) was low, but not low enough for the customer. Then, in October 1991, a special cause occurred. The company immediately investigated and identified a problem with a batch of raw material. The problem was easily corrected, but the conversation with the raw material provider led to a discussion about an additional improvement in the raw material. A series of designed experiments found the optimum composition, and the improved formulation was put into new product to be tested by the customer. The results were positive and the change was made standard for production. The improvement began to appear in March 1992, and the complaint level settled at 0.004 percent, a much more acceptable level. It was also sustainable because a fundamental improvement had been made to the process.*

This example is a good demonstration of process thinking and customer focus. Once the company and the customer understood the dynamics of their shared processes, action steps that improved the product were quickly implemented. The company and customer did not place blame or point fingers. They concentrated on resolving the problem, not on who caused it. The result was a partnership that improved process performance.

The team reacted appropriately to a special cause, starting a chain of events that ultimately reduced the reject rate by over 75 percent. They made good use of data by teaming with their customer to get numbers that would normally be inaccessible.

OPERATIONAL LEVEL

At the operational level, Statistical Thinking focuses on day-to-day processes such as those listed in Figure 6.6. Organizations practicing Statistical Thinking at this level use data for process improvement and to build in quality. Every worker understands the importance of reducing variation and is well-trained in the tools that help identify it. Key process outputs are monitored with time plots (run or control charts), and the plots help people make decisions.

✎   Simply knowing tools is not enough, though. They must be applied as part of a disciplined systematic approach to process improvement. The approach should include ongoing evaluation of

---

Examples of Operational Processes

- Manufacturing

- Order Entry

- Delivery

- Distribution

- Billing

- Collection

- Service

Figure 6.6 Operational Processes.

✎ TIP

Main Points to Consider at the Operational Level

- Use the CAP-Do variant of PDCA to diagnose the situation (see page 73).
- Form a team of stakeholders.
- Use flowcharts to diagnose and improve the process.
- Develop operational definitions.
- Listen to the customers.
- Develop key measures and plot the data over time.
- Eliminate special cause variation.
- Use Pareto charts to understand common causes of variation.

improvement opportunities, action plans when special causes are identified, and measures to insure that improvement gains are held.

The following case study serves two purposes. It discusses Statistical Thinking on an operational level, and it exemplifies how Statistical Thinking can be used on a personal level. Whether personal or professional, the key is to understand and reduce variation in the process.

CASE STUDY: STATISTICAL THINKING— A PERSONAL APPLICATION[3]

I was introduced to Statistical Thinking in October 1988, when I attended Heero Hacquebord's course, "Statistical Thinking for Leaders." I went into the course thinking that I already knew everything I needed to know about Statistical Process Control (SPC). I came out of the course with a new perspective, looking on statistics as a way of thinking about processes so we can learn how to improve them. I also found that I could never again be satisfied by looking at numbers without graphs.

✎ I immediately thought of all sorts of ways to apply this new knowledge at work and at home. One of my first applications was to control chart my weight and I have been doing so ever since. My enthusiasm, however, wasn't shared by my wife, Carolyn, an insulin-dependent diabetic since November 1976. I could see an obvious

---

✎ TIP

Display the data in ways to discover the nature of variation in the process.

- Plot the data over time. Always find a way to plot the key output data of a process over time. Whenever possible, develop a control chart of the data to identify the nature of the variation in the process.
- Build a histogram of the data. Look for patterns of variation in the histogram. A stable process will create a histogram with a consistent pattern. An unstable process will show different patterns over time or multiple peaks in the histogram.

application of control charts to her blood glucose level, which she was testing daily. No matter what my argument was, she wasn't interested.

Then in June 1994, something changed. The combination of pricking her finger up to four times per day to get blood, having laser surgery to repair diabetes-related eye damage, and having been sick so frequently during the winter of 1993/1994 got to her, and she agreed to be my guinea pig for applying Statistical Thinking.

The Objective

We started out with a few simple objectives. For Carolyn it was to reduce the pain and inconvenience of diabetes, and in particular, to regain her health and reduce her blood testing to once per day. My objective was to get her what she wanted. To do so I knew that we had to understand her "process" variation, gain control of it, and reduce that variation. It seemed like a simple problem; after all it should be just like a production process! It wasn't!

The Process

Carolyn is a "brittle" diabetic, due to the fact that she has little or no insulin production. In June 1994, her swings in blood glucose levels were high. The blood glucose range considered normal for non-diabetics is 70–120 milligrams/deciliter. It was not uncommon for Carolyn to vary from over 300 mg/dl to under 70 mg/dl (usually accompanied by an insulin reaction) within as few as 24 hours. I ran a regression analysis to try to determine the effect of insulin on her blood glucose and re-learned the futility of analyzing production records for correlations. The analysis indicated that increasing insulin increased blood glucose, an obvious error! In truth, the cause-and-effect was reversed. High blood glucose levels caused us to increase the insulin, not the other way around.

The Goal

Our main goal early in the project was to reduce glucose variation with an emphasis on reducing over-control. This was not a simple task because with diabetes there is no choice but to eat when blood glucose drops, and there is very little choice but to take extra insulin when blood glucose gets high. We needed to find a control condition for Carolyn's diabetes that would make her process more robust (insensitive to sources of variation).

Understanding Variation

Carolyn learned long ago that she had to take control of her own sickness and understand as much about it as she could. We dug into books and magazines and learned much about diabetes, including some of the mechanisms and key causes of blood glucose variation (food types, exercise, illness, infections, emotional stress, etc.) Bernstein (1984) identified a very important fact: The effect of any insulin on blood glucose usually diminishes as the blood glucose rises.

Near the end of the summer we began to make progress, but as we gained better control, Carolyn had more low blood glucose reactions, a serious potential problem. Low glucose tends to cause severe headaches and creates the potential for unconsciousness. The latter never happened, but the possible brain cell damage is very undesirable. However, we noticed that her reactions tended to occur when sleeping in the early morning.

To deal with this we developed a theoretical mathematical model of how her insulin levels would build up during a normal day. She was taking multiple shots per day of two kinds of insulin: Ultralente (long-acting, typically over 24 hours.) and Regular (short-acting, typically over 3 to 6 hours, to handle the immediate effect of meals). Our model indicated we could improve the overall uniformity of insulin if she delayed her last shot of Ultralente until about 8 P.M. rather than taking it at 6 P.M. with dinner. To coincide with the change we also delayed our dinnertime and were happy to see a reduction in early morning insulin reactions.

Finding Solutions

Knowing we could not eliminate the causes of high blood glucose, we needed a control strategy to bring down high blood glucose when it occurred. In the spirit of Statistical Thinking our first reaction to out-of-control signals was to ask, Why? and investigate. If the investigation called for an increase in insulin, we needed an adjustment plan.

The theory that seemed to fit best was that the blood glucose level really "wants" to be at some average level based on all the competing factors (insulin level, stress, illness/health, food intake, etc.). Due to the dynamics of the situation all these factors were changing simultaneously. At any moment in time no single value of either the insulin dose or blood glucose level really has meaning. Thus, we decided to use averages of each over a 24 to 48 hour period to determine how much to change the insulin doses to bring down high blood glucose. We developed an initial crude formula that worked well in dealing with high blood glucose levels in November 1994 and February 1995. We later developed a more fundamental theory that used differential equations and incorporated the non-linear effect of insulin on blood glucose.

Successful Results

The equation was successful in dealing with high blood glucose levels that occurred in May, June, July, August, and December 1995. We learned that it was important to keep the relative doses of Ultralente and Regular at about the same ratio (about 65–75 percent Ultralente) when applying the equation. We also found that we needed to apply the equation several times to counteract high blood glucose due to the dynamic nature of each situation. Using the equation in cases of low blood sugar was less effective since these instances often were accompanied by insulin reactions which generally required large doses of extra sugar to regain blood glucose levels.

The control charts (Figure 6.7 and Figure 6.8) show the results of Carolyn's blood glucose from June–August 1994, before we had gained much control, and after August 1994. The limits are based on one of the best periods of control: November 29, 1994, through January 3, 1995. The early data were taken usually as three to four readings a day. Beginning in January 1995 most data were taken once a day in the morning except during periods of high blood glucose, when more readings were needed. In general, analysis of the days with multiple readings failed to show any specific pattern in blood glucose levels throughout the day; thus, the data are graphed all together.

Benefits

There is clearly still plenty of room for improvement in controlling the complex process of Carolyn's blood glucose. However, we have

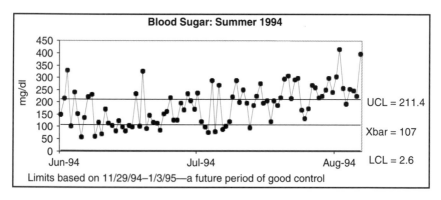

Figure 6.7   Blood Glucose—Summer 1994.

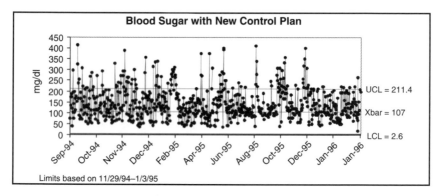

Figure 6.8   Blood Glucose with New Control Plan.

already obtained many benefits, most of which we believe can be directly attributed to our use of Statistical Thinking with control charts:

- *We met our objective of safely getting down to one blood glucose test a day. This was accomplished because we successfully reduced the variation in her process, making it possible to understand and predict within limits what was actually going on with her blood glucose.*

- *We learned much about the causes of Carolyn's high blood glucose (different foods, exercise, illness, infections, and especially emotional stress.)*

- *Carolyn takes 33 percent less insulin now than when we started and she also has lower blood glucose. We believe her body has adjusted to lower blood glucose and is more robust*

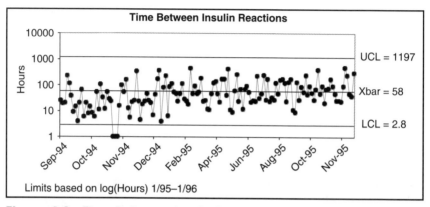

Figure 6.9 Time Between Insulin Reactions.

against fluctuations. In fact, Carolyn used to feel jittery at near normal blood glucose levels; she no longer feels that way.

- Carolyn was sick less often during the winters of 1994/1995 and 1995 to the time of this writing, compared to 1993/1994. (Winter 1994/1995: sick four times. 1995/present: sick two times. Winter 1993/1994: No hard data but memory recalls a frequency of an illness every one to three weeks.) In addition she has been much more energetic. High blood glucose tended to make her lethargic.

- A successful control strategy was developed for appropriately correcting high blood glucose with minimal over-control.

- The time between insulin reactions has improved; that is, the time between these reactions increased when compared to where it was when we first started to control the blood glucose. (Figure 6.9, Note: log of time between reactions was used due to the highly skewed nature of the time.)

- Carolyn was anticipating having a second laser surgery on her eye. Recent eye exams have indicated no need for surgery.

- We have developed some additional ideas for further control of Carolyn's diabetes. One thought to reduce the chance of night-time insulin reactions is for Carolyn to eat a small amount of food in the early morning (perhaps at 2 or 3 A.M.) Of course, that idea is not very popular with the subject and has been rejected at this time.

Lessons Learned

Beyond the tangible benefits of the control plan for Carolyn's health, we have also learned or reaffirmed some valuable lessons regarding Statistical Thinking and science:

- *A process has no regard for the specifications; it just does what it is capable of doing. There is no better evidence than this case of diabetes. The human internal insulin regulatory system controls blood glucose to within ±25 mg/dl. The best we've been able to get Carolyn's variation is ±104 mg/dl. Tampering only increased the variation.*
- *Statistical Thinking can help us develop theories as well as test them. We should remember to use all of our scientific/mathematical background to try to explain patterns in data.*
- *Chaos is alive and well and living in diabetes. It emphasizes the importance of creating robust processes that are less sensitive to sources of variation.*
- *The real value of control charts and Statistical Thinking is to help us learn about our processes. It is a serious fallacy to avoid introducing control charts to help understand a process just because we don't know how to control it. Simply plotting the data and separating special from common causes can be of great value. Failure to introduce the charts essentially guarantees continued ignorance of how to control the process.*
- *The human body is a marvelous creation that is extremely robust.*

While I was preparing this case study Carolyn pretty well summed up our results when she said, "I don't know what the data say about whether or not my diabetes improved, but I can tell you for sure I know it worked because I feel a lot better now than I did before we started!" As my friend, the late Ken Kotnour, once said in quoting Deming, "The customer doesn't always know what they need, but they will treasure it if you give it to them."

I should also add that Carolyn's physician, Dr. John Zenk, was very supportive of our efforts. We recommend that anyone who tries a similar approach should involve their physician, too.

Tom and Carolyn applied all aspects of Statistical Thinking. They recognized that turning food into glucose is a process and used that to full advantage in their improvement strategy. Instead of just studying numbers, they made concerted efforts to understand the process inputs and how their variation affected blood glucose. Statistical methods also played a role with the use of control charts and mathematical modeling to determine the proper insulin levels.

Once Tom and Carolyn had a better understanding of the variation in the process, they were able to apply techniques to reduce variation. The results were heartwarming: ". . . I can tell you for sure I know it worked because I feel a lot better now than I did before we started!" Can there be any better reason for applying Statistical Thinking in every part of our lives?

In summary, many people think that statistics and Statistical Thinking apply only at the operational level of an organization. The case studies clearly demonstrate the benefit of using this philosophy at all three levels—operational, managerial, and strategic. Although the types of processes are different at each level, the concepts of process, variation, and data reach across them all.

ENDNOTES

1. The authors would like to thank Bob Mitchell for providing this case history. Bob is a Senior Quality Specialist with 3M in St. Paul, MN. Prior to moving to St. Paul, Bob worked at 3M's facility in Hutchinson, MN.

2. This case history is courtesy of Galen Britz.

3. The authors would like to thank Tom Pohlen for this case history. Tom is a Senior Quality Engineering Specialist with 3M in Hutchinson, MN. A slightly expanded version of this case history appears in Britz et al. (1996).

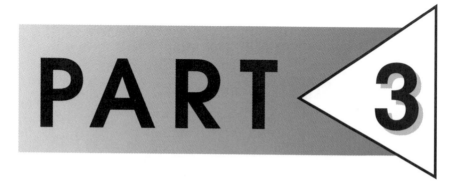

PART ◀ 3

HOW DO YOU APPLY STATISTICAL THINKING?

A Model for Applying Statistical Thinking 7

The previous two sections defined Statistical Thinking, explained its importance and discussed the fundamental concepts that make up Statistical Thinking. This section provides more specific tangible guidance on how to actually apply Statistical Thinking concepts and tools to real problems.

We begin with a model for applying Statistical Thinking, which provides a conceptual framework for the overall approach. This is followed by a real case study to illustrate a step-by-step approach to fundamental process improvement. This approach, called the *Process Improvement Strategy,* is a special case of the overall model.

Another case study illustrates a special case of the overall Statistical Thinking model, termed the *Problem Solving Strategy.* This approach is designed to address special causes, as opposed to fundamental process improvement.

A third case study demonstrates the application of both strategies in a business process environment subject to structural variation.

Used in conjunction, these strategies provide specific step-by-step approaches for both special cause and common cause problems. At each step the approaches list tools typically used in applications. References with detailed instruction in these tools appear at the end of the book; Chapter 11 and Chapter 13 discuss tools not included in the references.

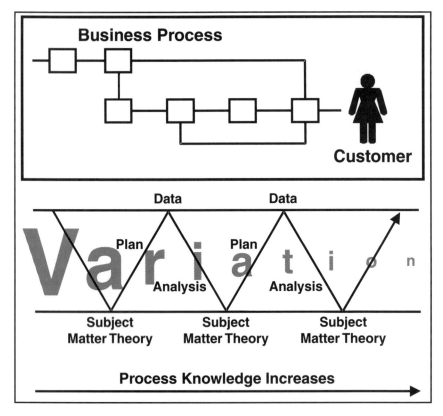

Figure 7.1   Statistical Thinking for Business Improvement.

THE STATISTICAL THINKING MODEL

Figure 7.1 depicts an overall model for applying Statistical Thinking to improve systems and processes. It is adapted from Hoerl and Snee (1995) and is an extension of Box, Hunter, and Hunter's (1978) "Conjecture → Design → Experiment → Analysis" model.

The model begins by identifying, documenting, and understanding the system or process itself, as represented by the graphic at the top of Figure 7.1. It then follows a repeating cycle of Subject matter theory → Plan → Data → Analysis.

Some degree of **subject matter theory** or knowledge almost always exists. This is everything we know about the process and usually is acquired from experience or academic study. The theory guides us in **planning** which data would be most helpful to validate or refine our theory. Once the **data** are obtained, they are **analyzed** using statistical approaches to account for the variation in the data, resulting in better understanding of the process. The analysis must be interpreted in light of existing subject matter theory to complete the cycle.

While the analysis may substantiate our basic theory, there are almost always unsuspected aspects that lead us to rethink or revise our theory to explain the data. Most real applications of Statistical Thinking are sequential studies involving a series of data gathering and theory revising steps.

Variation plays a major role in the cycle. Of course, there will always be variation generated by the process, but human variation permeates many other aspects of the model. There can be differences of opinion about what the process is and how it works. Different people may hold different beliefs about what is "known" about the process, i.e., the subject matter theory.

From a team dynamics perspective, if someone is just interested in implementing a solution or believes they will be embarrassed by the root cause of a problem, their ideas about the kind of data to collect and how it should be collected may be quite different than that of other team members. If the plan is not clearly communicated to people collecting the data, variation in the data collection process can obscure the results. Similarly, variation in test methods used in measurements adds an additional layer of "smoke" that prevents us from seeing the true situation. Different analyses of the same data may yield different conclusions, and finally, even reasonable people can disagree about the interpretation of an analysis and its meaning relative to subject matter theory.

Awareness of the variation is the first step in overcoming it. Continued cycles will provide more experience and better clarity about how to resolve differences and reduce variation, both traditional and non-traditional.

DIABETES AND THE STATISTICAL THINKING MODEL

The case study involving Carolyn Pohlen's diabetes from Chapter 6 is a good example of the Statistical Thinking model. The author, Tom Pohlen, noted that the process was Carolyn's regulation of blood glucose (her diabetes). Their subject matter theory came from reading (they knew what her blood glucose levels should be) and experience (they knew the approximate range over which the level actually varied).

Tom's initial plan was to gather data to try to correlate insulin to blood glucose using regression analysis. His analysis yielded an unexpected result: increasing insulin increases blood glucose. Since this disagreed with his subject matter knowledge, he knew that either the theory was wrong or there was a problem with the data. Further reflection caused him to reconsider how the "happenstance" data were collected and he revised his approach for future data collection.

In their next loop through the Statistical Thinking model, they gained more subject matter knowledge, learning about the non-linear relationship between insulin and blood glucose and developing a mathematical model to predict insulin levels. Additional data turned up another unexpected result: low glucose reactions, which the analysis showed usually occurred in the early morning.

This added to their subject matter knowledge and they looped through the cycle again by using the mathematical model to change the time of Carolyn's last daily shot. The data and analysis confirmed the improvement.

As is typically the case, their knowledge about the process, and consequently their ability to improve it, increased with each loop through the Statistical Thinking Model. Continued study of the data and subject matter literature led Tom to develop predictive equations to determine how much insulin to give Carolyn. Ongoing monitoring of the data from this approach led to several discoveries and fine-tuning of the equation.

The primary variation in this case was from the process itself. The tremendous variation in Carolyn's blood glucose was a significant complication and required careful interpretation to prevent overreaction. Another potential source of variation is the variation in measuring blood glucose and the amount of insulin injected. From a broader perspective, variation in improvement approaches led to a 5½ year time lag between Tom's first encounter with Statistical Thinking and Carolyn's willingness to give it a try.

THE STATISTICAL THINKING MODEL, THE SCIENTIFIC METHOD, AND PDCA

This model of Statistical Thinking can be viewed as an adaptation of the Scientific Method and Plan-Do-Check-Act (PDCA). In its simplest form, the *scientific method* begins with a stated *hypothesis* about a phenomenon. An *experiment* is conducted to test the hypothesis, and *observation* of the results confirms or disproves the hypothesis. In application, of course, this method will also be sequential, since observations from one experiment may cause us to revise our hypothesis, and lead to another experiment to evaluate the revised hypothesis. PDCA, depicted in Figure 7.2 and discussed on page 72, is a systematic, sequential approach to improvement, developed by Shewhart and popularized by Deming.

Statistical Thinking incorporates the basic scientific method approach of developing subject matter theory and gathering data to evaluate and revise it, and the sequential approach of PDCA, as well as the iterative nature of both. However, there are two fundamental differences in emphasis: *process* and *variation*. These are implicit in both the scientific method and PDCA, but many people apply them without recognizing these two important concepts. The model described in Figure 7.1 makes them explicit via the flowchart to represent the process and the shrinking word "Variation" to recognize the role of variation and the goal of reducing it.

In summary, the key aspects of applying Statistical Thinking illustrated by this model and the case study are:

- Work occurs through a process or series of processes (system). To improve the results we must improve the process.
- Applications typically begin with subject matter knowledge, not data. Subject matter knowledge helps determine the type of data we need to improve the process, although we should be careful that our assumptions about subject matter knowledge don't bias the questions we ask or the data we collect.
- Data are the link between the process and our knowledge. They allow us to test and generate hypotheses as the data are evaluated with statistical tools to account for variation.

- Statistical Thinking applications are generally iterative. New information is discovered at each step, leading to revision and fine-tuning of our theories. Revised theories lead to new questions to be answered with data, hence the cycle continues. Overall knowledge increases with each iteration through the cycle.

To conclude, Figure 7.1 is a generic model for applying Statistical Thinking. While this is important for keeping the big picture in mind it is often useful to have a more systematic approach when approaching specific applications. The next two chapters discuss two strategies: process improvement and problem solving. The Process Improvement Strategy is used to improve the fundamental capability of the process. The Problem Solving Strategy is used to identify and respond to special causes.

Step by step "cookbooks" can be dangerous if the practitioner lacks a good conceptual understanding of the big picture. Therefore, we recommend that readers strive to thoroughly understand the Statistical Thinking model prior to using the step-by-step strategies outlined in the next two chapters.

Plan-Do-Check-Act

Statistical Thinking should be used in conjunction with Plan-Do-Check-Act (PDCA) cycles. PDCA is a continuous improvement model developed by W. A. Shewhart to systematically minimize process variation. In the context of experimentation, for example, researchers **plan** an experiment to test a theory, **do** the experiment, **check** the results of the experiment, and **act** on the results. As the name suggests, there are four major stages to this model:

Plan: Define the problem and the potential causes of the problem. Develop a strategy to improve the process.

Do: Implement the plan to improve the process, ensuring that the new process is documented and supported by the people who use the process.

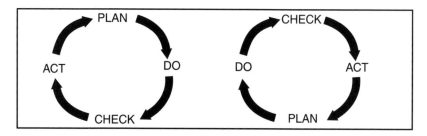

Figure 7.2 PDCA and CAP-Do.

Check: Confirm the effectiveness of the implemented plan by verifying the results.

Act: Adopt or modify the plan as needed to achieve the intended result. Document the revised process.

PDCA symbolizes the principle of iteration in problem solving. The process has only four steps, but they are repeated many times. One advantage to this approach is that as improvement strategies are implemented, quick feedback can be obtained about the effectiveness of the plan. The direction and magnitude of changes can be quantified, resulting in improved products and services.

CAP-Do vs. PDCA

When teams have difficulty deciding where to begin applying the PDCA approach, an assessment of the current process is often a good starting point. It is often helpful to begin with the check step to identify the major issues. Using the check phase, followed by act-plan-do can result in decisions based on current process performance. Like PDCA, CAP-Do is comprised of four stages.

Check: Identify current process problems that inhibit desired results; determine the scope and the key players of the project.

Act: Implement obvious changes to drive the process closer to desired results. Determine the best improvement approach.

Plan: Determine what is desired for the future. Develop the plan.

Do: Implement the plan to drive the process to the futuristic goal, ensuring that the new process is documented and supported by the persons who use the process.

The Process
Improvement Strategy

The following case study illustrates the application of the overall Statistical Thinking model to process improvement. It is adapted from *The Quest for Higher Quality—The Deming Prize and Quality Control,* by Ricoh, Ltd. See Imai (1986) for more details.

CASE STUDY: RESIN VARIATION REDUCTION
An Application of the Process Improvement Strategy

A production team at Ricoh's Numazu plant was in charge of production and inspection of raw materials used to make plain paper copier (PPC) toner. Their objective was to produce consistent resin quality and volume through daily operation of a sequential chemical process.

A consistent, perplexing problem involved a yield that was determined by the ratio $\frac{Actual\ Output}{Theoretical\ Output}$. The yield regularly exceeded 100 percent, a technical impossibility, and the team believed that values calculated over 100 percent were due to excessive variation somewhere in the process.

Figure 8.1 contains a macro-level flowchart of the process. Each lot of raw material goes through two processing steps, then is divided in half. The two halves go through steps three and four separately, are weighed, and packed into large drums.

After reaching a common understanding of the overall process flow, the team created time plots, such as in Figure 8.2, to study process stability. They began by investigating the period in the middle

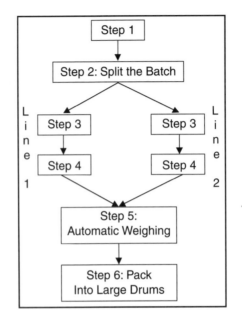

Figure 8.1   Flowchart of Resin Process.

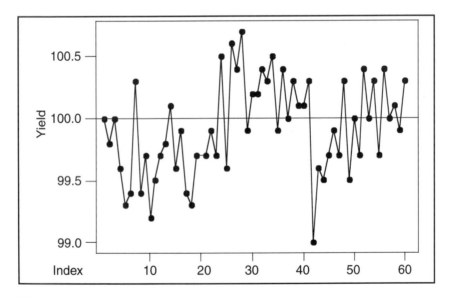

Figure 8.2   Resin yield over time.

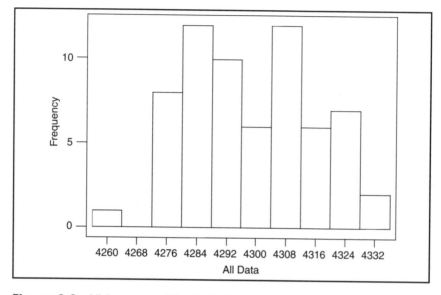

Figure 8.3   Histogram of Resin Output.

of the graph, where most values were above 100 percent, and found that a mechanical problem, since repaired, was the root cause.

The actual process output obviously was critical in the equation, so the next step was to plot a histogram of recent output data, shown in Figure 8.3. The unusual pattern, with peaks at 4,284 kg and 4,308 kg, suggested two underlying distributions combined in the data. Recalling that each batch is split in half after step two, the team stratified the data by line and made individual histograms for the two batches, as shown in Figure 8.4. These clearly revealed that output from line two was consistently lower than the output from line 1. It also showed evidence of further bimodality in line two, but the team chose not to pursue this.

The team also investigated the needs of their customers to determine a target and allowable tolerance. They agreed on a target of 4,300 kg, with a tolerance of plus or minus 5 kg, as their objective. These standards are noted on Figure 8.4. Clearly, major improvements were still needed.

The team brainstormed potential causes for the resin variation, documented their collective thinking in the cause-and-effect diagram in Figure 8.5, and highlighted areas which could explain the consistent difference between the paired batches. The highest priority

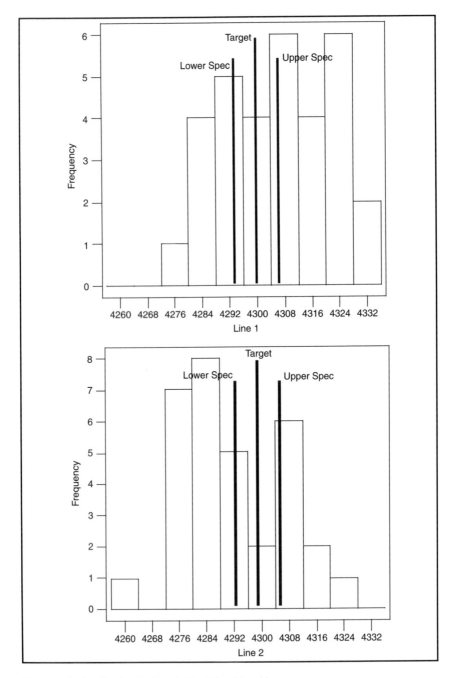

Figure 8.4 Resin Output Stratified by Line.

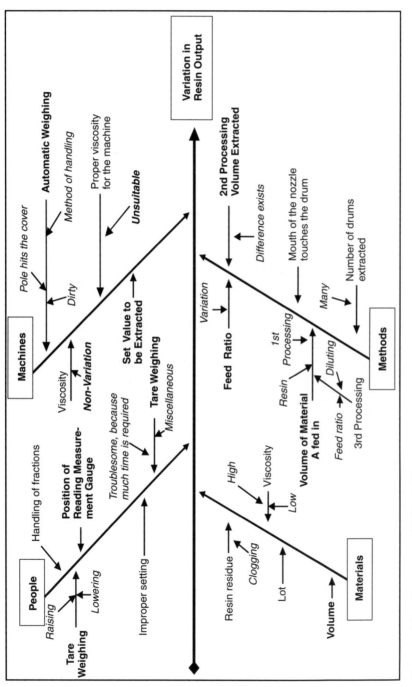

Figure 8.5 Cause-and-Effect Diagram.

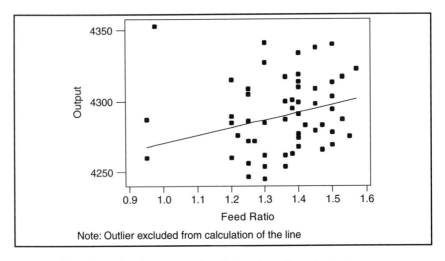

Figure 8.6   Scatter Diagram for Output vs. Feed Ratio.

issues selected by the team were the procedure for dividing the resin after the second processing step (most likely to be related to differences in the paired batches), the solvent feed ratio, and the weighing processes, both final (automatic) and in-process (manual).

While addressing the first issue, the team noticed that some resin remained in the reaction tank after the dividing step, meaning that the second batch had less material than the first, and consequently, lower output. A subsequent change to the dividing procedure ensured an even split of the reaction tank, a conclusion borne out by data demonstrating no detectable difference between the two batches.

Despite this improvement, there was still too much variation, so the team's focus moved to the next highest priority item on their cause and effect diagram, the solvent feed ratio. A scatter plot of feed ratio versus output (Figure 8.6) hinted at a relationship between the two, with increasing ratios associated with higher output measurements[1]. This contradicted the team's subject matter knowledge, since they did not believe such a relationship could exist. Further investigation showed that the ratio measurement was affected by how long the solvent sat in the tank. The team changed the procedure to ensure that the solvent had stabilized prior to measurement. Subsequent data demonstrated reduced variation in the

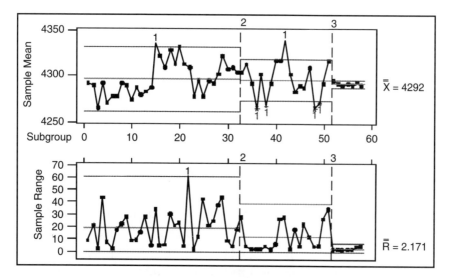

Figure 8.7 Output Control Charts—Average and Range.

feed ratio, and the relationship between measured output and feed ratio disappeared.

The output variation was still not at the desired levels, however, and the team felt that further improvement was possible. Hence, they embarked on another round of variation countermeasures. They addressed the weighing processes next and noticed that the in-process manual method depended on accurate reading of a particular line on the scale. They also noticed that people of different heights read it at different angles, and consequently, got different readings. To remedy this source of variation the team changed the position of the line so that everyone saw it at the same angle, reducing in-process measurement variation.

In addition, the team found problems with the design and alignment of the final, automatic scale. These were corrected with a new design for the scale's protective cover and new procedures for checking the alignment on a regular basis.

As can be seen in Figure 8.7, which displays a control chart of the average batch outputs, the variation was significantly reduced, meeting the team's variation objective. While the desired average of 4,300 kg was not obtained, the resulting average of about 4,292 kg was considered more than adequate, given the reduction *in variation, which was the team's main objective. As an added benefit, the process improvements resulted in a reduction of resin viscosity variation as well.*

To standardize on the improvements, and prevent backsliding, the team:

- *prepared a resin extraction procedures manual.*
- *prepared a solvent insertion procedures manual.*
- *revised the manual for synthesizing resin.*
- *set a schedule for periodic assessment of the automatic weighing process.*

Several important points illustrated in this case study are worth repeating:

- Many improvement projects focus on reducing variation around the average as opposed to changing the average. A large standard deviation is often the key issue.
- The measurement process is often a root cause of other problems. A lot of money has been spent on new materials or equipment, when the measurement process was the real culprit.
- Repeated cycles through the Statistical Thinking model are usually necessary for major permanent improvements.
- While each Statistical Thinking tool is valuable, it is their combined use in a disciplined overall approach that leads to bottom line improvements.

THE PROCESS IMPROVEMENT STRATEGY

The resin variation reduction case closely follows the key steps in applying the Statistical Thinking model to process improvement. These steps, along with the tools typically used at each step, are shown in Figure 8.8, from Hoerl and Snee (1995). This is similar to other published step-by-step improvement approaches, such as those in Gaudard, Coates, and Freeman (1991), the Xerox Corporation (1993), and Joiner (1994). The list of tools is certainly not exhaustive, nor is it implied that each must be used for every application.

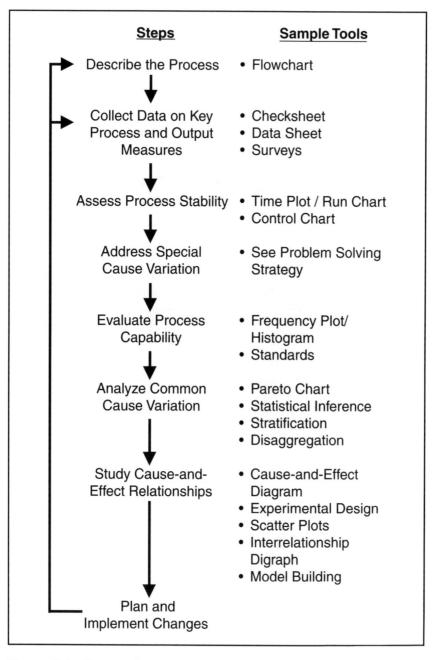

Figure 8.8 Process Improvement Strategy.

The strategy is generic in nature, and it is not intended to be followed religiously to the smallest detail. In addition, there must be some prerequisites to beginning this strategy, such as clearly defining the overall scope and objectives. The following pages illustrate and discuss the steps in the process improvement strategy.

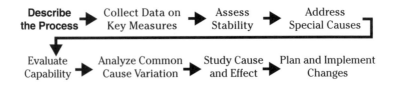

Describe the Process

The purpose of this step is to document the process involved, typically with flowcharts. The mere act of creating a flowchart can expose issues and questions about how the process is actually performed. These questions can lead to immediate improvements as a standardized process is developed. Opportunity flowcharts[2] can also identify process steps that do not add value to the product or service. Non-value added steps are generally performed because of constraints and inefficiencies in the process or fear that something may go wrong, and represent opportunities for improvement. Finally, flowcharts can serve as communication vehicles for people who are not intimately familiar with the process.

Most of the case studies in this book began with fairly high level or "macro" flowcharts. In the resin case study, the flowchart immediately suggested a stratification of the output data by line.

Flowcharting of administrative and service processes is particularly important, since we cannot physically see the process at work. We may also wish to benchmark, or compare how we perform this process to the way others, such as competitors or recognized authorities, perform the same process.

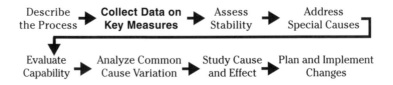

Collect Data on Key Process and Output Measures

Understanding the current situation is often the best place to begin study of a process. A flowchart is a good place to start, and the next logical step is to collect data to see how the process is currently performing. Data can include inputs, outputs, and key process variables that either predict how well the product or service will work for customers, or assess the health of the process itself.

Measured or counted data, such as yield, output, or time to answer, are typically recorded on paper or electronic data sheets. The complaint and monthly sales data in Chapter 6 were collected this way. When the data are gathered from people, surveys or questionnaires are often used. Categorical data, where the data are in one of two or more categories, are typically recorded on a checksheet. Such a checksheet could have been used in the complaint case to record the specific reason for each individual complaint.

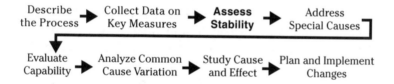

Assess Process Stability

At this point, it is critically important to assess the stability of the process, typically with run charts, i.e., plots of data over time, or control charts. Assessing stability is important because it will influence the next step in the improvement process. In addition, many common statistical methods, such as t-tests and ANOVA, are not valid on unstable processes.

Stability generally implies lack of special causes, in which case we need to study and understand the common cause structure, so we can change the underlying process. Instability generally implies the presence of special causes, which we should identify and address.

Note that stability does not imply that the process is performing satisfactorily, only that it is consistent over time.

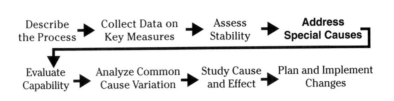

Address Special Cause Variation

Large special causes are generally few in number and can be related to specific events rather than being a fundamental part of the system. Harmful special causes are typically easier to identify and eliminate than common cause variation, and generally produce the most dramatic short-term improvements. In other words, fixing special causes often represents "picking the low hanging fruit," at least in comparison to changing the process fundamentally. The elimination of special causes also results in a stable process, which makes study of the common cause structure much easier.

While most of the resin improvement team's work revolved around reducing common cause variation, early on they found a special cause that temporarily made nearly all of their yields exceed 100 percent. After that was addressed, they were able to get a much clearer picture of common cause variation.

Note that the approach for addressing special causes is different than for addressing common causes. The Problem Solving strategy, as depicted in Figure 9.5 on page 99 [from Hoerl and Snee (1995)] is the overall strategy for identifying and eliminating root causes.

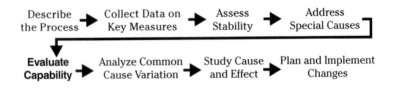

Evaluate Process Capability

With stable processes, the next step is to evaluate process capability against process goals or specifications. Most processes have some sort of standard: a goal or specification to define what we want. The standards are often external, such as customer needs or the performance of a competitor, and aren't necessarily related to what the process can produce. Many manufacturing processes have a target and specifications that define minimum and maximum acceptable values for a process output, such as the resin team's 4,300 ± 5 kg. Managerial and service processes often operate with goals, such as the 97.5 percent on-time delivery goal in Chapter 5.

This step is intended to determine whether the process, given its current average and standard deviation, can consistently meet the goals and specifications imposed on it. The evaluation is typically done with histograms and standards. In the case of two-sided specifications, a histogram with standards noted on it allows us to see how close the actual average is to the target and if the observed variation will fit within the desired limits. With a one-sided goal, we can see how frequently the process is likely to meet the goal. This helps diagnose whether we have an issue with the average, variation, or both.

People often use process capability indices such as C_p or C_{pk} to quantify process capability in manufacturing processes. However, we caution users against over-reliance on one-number summaries since they may provide an incomplete picture of the process. For more information, see Gunter (1989 and 1991).

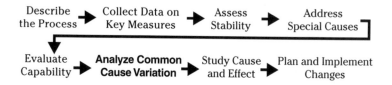

Analyze Common Cause Variation

If the problems that created the improvement project still remain after eliminating special causes, the process will likely have been found not capable in the previous step. Improvement then means attacking common cause variation.

As noted in Chapter 5, common cause variation affects (and hence we should study, preferably with graphs) all the data.

Histograms are often good places to start, as the resin team discovered when they saw two peaks in their output histogram.

The primary goal of this step, though, is to isolate sources of variation. Stratification to compare subsets of data in search of differences, disaggregation to focus on a particular subprocess, and Pareto charts to look for a small number of causes accounting for the majority of occurrences (often referred to as the 80/20 rule) are all helpful. Statistical inference, such as t-tests, ANOVA, and regression can numerically verify the results of stratification and Pareto analysis.

After observing the two peaks in their histogram, the resin team's subject matter knowledge led them to identify the divided batches as a likely cause for this shape. They acted on their knowledge by stratifying and plotting separate histograms for each batch. Had they been dealing with attribute or categorical data, such as a number of defect types or causes of equipment downtime, they might have used a Pareto chart to identify the most frequently occurring causes.

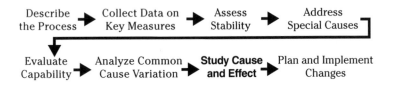

Study Cause-and-Effect Relationships

The analysis of common cause variation in the previous step helps narrow the focus of the problem. This step leads us to root causes. It is tempting to implement solutions early in the problem solving process, and it's a good idea if the solutions are truly obvious. If not, it is better to wait until root causes have been determined, to avoid the potential of implementing multiple expensive "solutions" that don't make anything better.

A variety of tools can help identify cause and effect relationships. Cause-and-effect diagrams (also known as fishbone or Ishikawa diagrams) help organize potential root causes. Scatter plots can show trends in data, and design of experiments (DOE) with associated model building can develop equations to explain and predict the behavior of a process. The resin team used cause-and-effect diagrams and scatter plots in their improvement efforts.

At managerial or strategic levels of the organization, interrelationship digraphs can help determine causal direction of relationships. For example, does A cause B, or does B cause A? (see Chapter 13 for more detail.)

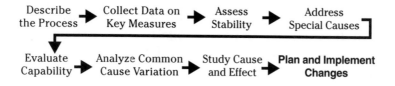

Plan and Implement Changes

As understanding of causal relationships is developed, it becomes easier to determine what changes would improve the process. Several counter-measures were taken to reduce between-batch variation as a result of the cause and effect relationships, including changing the batch splitting procedure, modifying the solvent ratio measurement method, and revising work standards.

Planning the changes cannot be overemphasized, since they may affect many people in unexpected ways, including how they do their work, who they work with, and even the very nature of the work. Major changes should be piloted on a smaller scale, if possible, and people issues, such as the psychology of change, should be considered.

It should be noted that in process improvement, several changes are typically needed to obtain the desired performance, as indicated in Figure 8.8 by the loop back to the beginning of the process. Radical changes may warrant a revision to the original flowchart to document the new process. Other changes may require the loop to go back only to the data collection step.

THE PROCESS IMPROVEMENT STRATEGY AND THE STATISTICAL THINKING MODEL

As previously noted, the Process Improvement Strategy in Figure 8.8 should be viewed as a more specific and detailed example of the Statistical Thinking model depicted in Figure 7.1. The Process Improvement Strategy begins with *Describe the Process.* This generally uses a knowledge-based tool, the flowchart, rather than a data-based tool, and relies on subject matter theory. The next several steps use this knowledge to generate data, analyses, and actions, which further the subject matter knowledge.

Analyze Common Cause Variation and *Study Causal Relationships* often require several iterations through this same cycle. Each iteration is guided by the latest revision to our theories based on the most recent data collected. *Plan and Implement Changes* is strictly knowledge-based, and needs to be followed with a data gathering step to ensure that the changes produced the desired results.

Finally, the Process Improvement Strategy incorporates the key elements of the Statistical Thinking approach:

- Improving results by improving the process
- Diagnosing and reducing variation
- Synergy between subject matter, theory, and data
- A sequential approach

ENDNOTES

1. If you think the relationship is weak, the authors agree. Nevertheless, the team was able to use the information to learn more about their process.
2. See Scholtes, et al. (1996).

The Problem Solving Strategy

The Process Improvement Strategy is designed for fundamental process improvement. However, there are times when specific problems or special causes need to be solved. The following case study shows the application of the Statistical Thinking model to problem solving. It is followed by a step-by-step approach specifically designed for problem solving.

Note that a number of tools are discussed in the case history. Readers unfamiliar with these tools can learn more about them in Chapter 11 and Chapter 13.

CASE STUDY: RESOLVING CUSTOMER COMPLAINTS OF BABY WIPE FLUSHABILITY[1]

The Super-Wipe brand of baby wipes had been a very profitable business for Acme Baby Care Company. The product provided good performance in cleaning infants during diaper changing, and it was sold at a cost considerably lower than the leading brands. A key selling point was the wipes' flushability. Unlike competitive baby wipes that had to be disposed of through trash removal or diaper services, Super-Wipe could be flushed down the toilet, preventing customers from having to keep soiled wipes around the house. The ability to flush was achieved through use of a proprietary mix of natural and synthetic fibers.

This rosy picture turned into a disaster when the business team learned that the consumer relations department was being flooded with calls and letters complaining that Super-Wipe was not flushing properly. This was particularly perplexing since Acme had performed extensive septic system tests prior to introducing Super-Wipe, and it had passed with flying colors. A Super-Wipe Action Team (SWAT) of technical experts from research & development and manufacturing was assembled to fix the problem quickly. Consumer relations, marketing, and sales worked on a parallel path to maintain distributors' and consumers' faith in the product.

The team had a diversity of expertise in areas such as synthetic fibers, natural fibers, processing chemicals, and manufacturing technology. Despite extreme managerial pressure to fix the problem before it resulted in a total marketing disaster, they initially made little progress, as all experts wished to pursue solutions in their individual areas of expertise. A turning point occurred when the team jointly recognized that they really did not understand the problem well, and would need to work cooperatively, using a disciplined approach, to solve the problem.

While the manufacturing process was well understood by the team, they still developed a flowchart to serve as a base of reference, and facilitate communication. Consumer relations provided flushability complaint data and the team plotted the run chart in Figure 9.1. This plot clearly showed that complaints had increased dramatically. Pinpointing the exact onset was difficult because of the lag between when the product was manufactured, when it reached retail stores, when it was purchased by consumers, when it was actually used, and when a complaint was received. However, stratification by manufacturing plant revealed a key piece of information: the problem was primarily associated with one factory.

The obvious step at this point was to identify what caused the increase in complaints. Since most team members had strong opinions on this issue, the team decided to capture all the ideas through a structured brainstorming session. This was followed by lengthy discussions of the various theories about the root cause, including new synthetic fibers that had recently been added to the product, various chemicals being used, as well as some current process conditions. Another theory was that the problem was related to introduction of low-volume toilets, and not associated with the product at all.

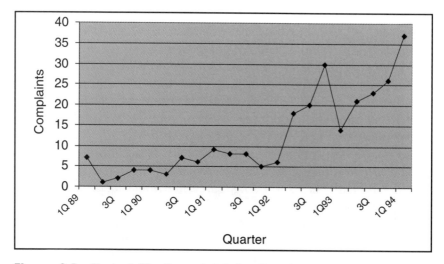

Figure 9.1 Flushability Complaints by Quarter.

Since no clear consensus emerged on a most probable cause, the team used multi-voting to identify the following highest priority items:

- *New synthetic fibers*
- *Use of the chemical X-Pro*
- *Chemical surfactants used in the process*
- *Trace chemicals in the plant water supply*

All except the plant water supply were known to have changed around the time the complaints began to increase. X-Pro was a chemical added to the wet synthetic/natural fiber mixture to enhance strength of the wipe and to aid mixing. It allowed the process to run faster, resulting in increased productivity. Surfactants are chemical soaps that were added to the product to reduce surface tension, making it feel smoother and clean better.

Another complicating factor was that there was no agreed-upon method of measuring flushability, hence it was not easy to determine if the product was actually defective. The long-term septic system tests performed prior to introducing the product were not considered practical to use on a routine basis, so the team added a fifth high priority action item: develop a simple, repeatable, flushability test.

The team split into five task teams, with some overlapping membership, each pursuing one action item. The flushability measurement team obviously had the highest urgency, since progress on the other four would be held up until flushability could be quantified. To observe the problem first hand, they visited the homes of some people who had complained. After observing flushing for several days, and even opening septic tanks, they concluded that Super-Wipe was definitely not flushing as designed. The problem could not be blamed on low volume toilets. In addition, some fibers were seen floating indefinitely, even after the wipe had broken apart. This was very surprising, since the fibers were denser than water, and should have sunk.

This discovery piqued everyone's interest and led the task team to consider whether the problem was flushability—clogging of plumbing and septic systems due to the wipe not breaking apart when flushed, or simply floating fibers. The team began developing both a flushability test and a float test. The final flushability test measured how long the wipe took to disintegrate in water with mild agitation, while the float test measured the percent of fibers still floating after a fixed time of immersion in water. Once these tests were developed and documented, baseline data on Super-Wipe and its competitors was gathered. Figure 9.2 shows histograms for flushability; the floatation results were similar. Clearly, Super-Wipe had a quantifiable problem relative to competition.

At this point, the other teams became more active. The synthetic fiber team designed an experiment to study the effect of changing the amounts of three types of synthetic fiber as shown in Figure 9.3². *The experiment showed that while changing the fiber amounts may have had a small effect, it was not the reason for the great disparity relative to competition.*

The X-Pro team, meanwhile, learned from the vendor that X-Pro should not be added to a wet fiber mixture. Instead, it should be sprayed on in a later processing step. They could not, however, explain how this might cause flushability or floating problems. Nevertheless, the team got approval to order spraying equipment and planned to experiment with removal of X-Pro in the meantime. Reality set in when the plant would not allow experiments to remove X-Pro because of productivity concerns.

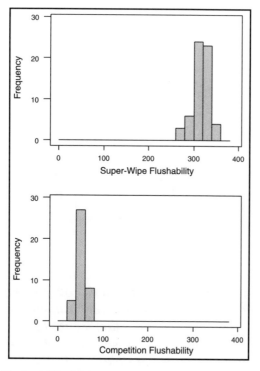

Figure 9.2 Flushability Histogram.

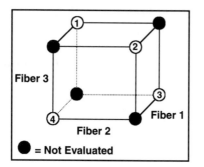

Figure 9.3 Experimental Conditions.

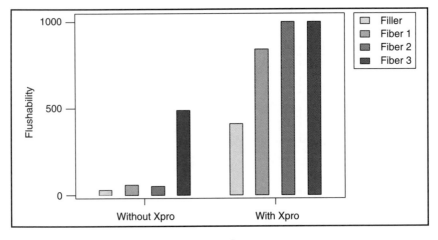

Figure 9.4 Additional Laboratory Data.

The water supply and surfactant teams both ran experiments with their ingredients and found no impact on flushability or floating.

At this point, process of elimination focused suspicion on X-Pro. While waiting for a shutdown for installation of the spraying equipment, one team member began tinkering in the lab with various fibers and X-Pro, producing the data in Figure 9.4. It appeared that X-Pro was a cause of the problem and there were possible differences between fibers as well, although the effect of adding X-Pro was not the same for all fiber types. These data caused some members of the SWAT to reconsider fiber as a potential root cause, while others were skeptical of the data because of the difficulty of exactly reproducing process in the laboratory. The result was a great deal of disagreement and minimal progress.

The logjam was quickly broken when the process experienced a mechanical problem. When it was repaired, the flushability and float numbers showed significant improvement, operating at about the same level as competition. Upon investigating this special cause, a team member discovered an error in an equipment setting. Water was being pumped into the process instead of X-Pro. Faced with this evidence, the entire team was convinced X-Pro addition in the wet state was the culprit, and the spraying equipment was installed.

When X-Pro was sprayed according to the vendor's instructions, Super-Wipe had neither flushability nor runability problems. To protect against reoccurrence, the plant continued flushability testing on a periodic basis. Float tests were discontinued since it was a more time-consuming test, and because floating only occurred with flushability problems.

Several important points illustrated in this case study are worth repeating:

- Experts tend to suggest solutions even before the problem has been documented and agreed upon. As in this case, careful documentation of the problem and a disciplined approach are critical to effective problem solving.
- Difficulty in obtaining accurate, meaningful measurements is a common problem; hence, validation of the measurement process often needs to be addressed early in the project.
- Working with customers to observe actual product use is often invaluable in problem solving.
- Teamwork requires more than a collection of experts. Each member must be aligned to a common set of goals and work cooperatively to achieve them.
- Some experiments succeed by not showing any new results. While the fiber team's experiment didn't show large effects due to changing the amount of each fiber, they were able to rule out fiber as a reason for the special cause that increased the complaints.
- Instituting permanent procedures to test for flushability was a critical step to rapidly detect reoccurrence of the problem. Without this step, the same problems tend to be "solved" over and over again. This is particularly true in organizations that value heroic "fire-fighting" efforts more than planning and prevention.

THE PROBLEM SOLVING STRATEGY

The flushability case study bears some similarities to the resin variation reduction case study, which utilized the Process Improvement Strategy. They both employed sequential approaches, viewed work as a process, made use of several tools, integrated data collection and analysis with subject matter knowledge, and recognized the importance of understanding and reducing variation. Upon closer examination, however, there is a critical difference. The process improvement case study (resin variation reduction) developed deeper understanding of the *normal behavior* of the process, so that it could be *improved fundamentally.* The baby-wipe case, on the other hand, identified and diagnosed the root cause of *abnormal behavior* so that the process could be *returned to normal.* We refer to the latter approach as problem solving.

Process improvement is required to take a stable process (one with only common cause variation) to a new level. Problem solving is required to deal with the special causes in an unstable process. Since special causes are, by definition, not an inherent part of the process, they can generally be addressed without fundamental process change. For this reason, it makes sense to address the special causes first, then fundamentally improve the process. This sequence is depicted in Figure 8.8, where problem solving is applied to special cause variation prior to the more in-depth process improvement steps.

The overall approach to problem solving is depicted in Figure 9.5. As noted in the Process Improvement Strategy, the problem solving approach is used only after describing the process, gathering data on key process measures and outputs, and determining that the process is unstable. The next several pages illustrate and discuss each step in the Problem Solving Strategy.

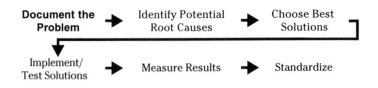

Document the Problem

Since the emphasis in problem solving is identifying root causes of abnormal behavior, we focus on the abnormal behavior, rather than the overall process. This requires thoughtful documentation

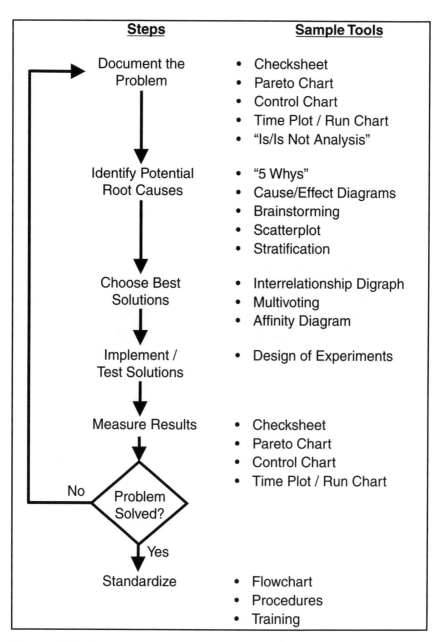

Figure 9.5 Problem Solving Strategy.

of the problem and all related symptoms. In fact, careful, thorough documentation may be the most important step. The same run or control chart that detected the special cause can help us diagnose exactly when it occurred, and whether the change was gradual or sudden. With Super-Wipe, the run chart of customer complaints revealed the specific months when complaints increased. This significantly narrowed the list of potential root causes. Checksheets and Pareto charts may be used to reveal changes in attribute data.

One systematic method for documenting and isolating specific problems is Is/Is Not analysis. For example, the baby-wipe flushability problem was at one Acme plant but not at others, although it could have been. This suggested that the root cause was related to a difference between this one plant and the others, rather than a circuit-wide cause, such as common raw materials used by all. This is equivalent to identifying special causes outside of a time-based context. This particular Acme plant was a special cause. Such detailed documentation is extremely helpful in suggesting and testing various theories that attempt to explain the abnormal behavior.

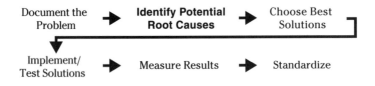

Identify Potential Root Causes

As with process improvement, it is important to identify root causes before implementing solutions. Once the problem is thoroughly documented, it is easier to identify potential root causes. A common mistake is to attempt to solve a poorly defined or poorly documented problem. Structured brainstorming is a useful tool to formally capture a diverse team's opinions without discussion or debate, as used in the baby-wipe case. The Five whys, that is asking "Why?" as many as five times can also help dig beneath symptoms to get to root cause. Some previously mentioned tools are also helpful in suggesting potential root causes. These include a mixture of knowledge-based tools, such as cause-and-effect diagrams, and data-based tools, such as stratification and scatter plots.

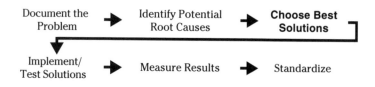

Choose Best Solutions

Often a large number of plausible causes will be identified. The next step is to gather data, if possible, to identify the most likely cause and select potential solutions. Some solutions may address several potential causes. The key is to get the whole team aligned on a common path forward. This prevents people from pursuing independent solutions in a haphazard manner, which often makes matters worse. Several "soft" tools are helpful here, including affinity diagrams to create logical categories of causes, interrelationship digraphs to determine the causal direction (both discussed in Chapter 13), and multi-voting to give all team members an equal opportunity to provide input. Of course, subject matter knowledge still must be used to ensure that the most probable causes are identified, rather than the most popular.

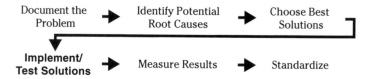

Implement/Test Solutions

If the high-priority potential solutions are relatively easy to implement, they are generally implemented fully. In other cases, such as the baby-wipes, full implementation would be quite expensive. For example, replacing all of the low-cost fibers with more expensive ones could have cost hundreds of thousands of dollars. In these situations, it is much more sensible to test the solutions on a trial basis. Experimental design techniques are the best known approach to studying the effects of several factors with a minimal investment of time, money, and effort. Using this approach, the impact of three suspect fibers was evaluated quickly and at a very low cost. While none proved to be the root cause of flushability problems, explicitly revealing this fact enabled the team to move on to other potential solutions.

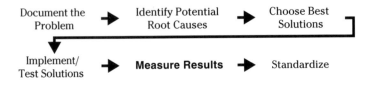

Measure Results

It is often tempting to declare success after implementing a proposed solution prior to obtaining evidence that the problem has actually been solved. Doing this too many times can strain people's credibility.

After solutions have been implemented, it is important to quantify and document the results. Analysis of designed experiments includes a number of graphical methods for interpreting results of trial changes. Permanent changes are often evaluated with run or control charts if the data are continuous, such as money or cycle time. With attribute data such as causes for complaints or injuries, Pareto charts indicate whether the solution actually solved the problem.

If the problem has not been solved, we need to loop back to select and try the next highest-priority potential causes. As was the case for baby-wipe complaints, we may finally find the true cause by a process of elimination.

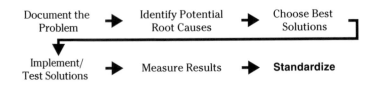

Standardize

Even if the problem was solved, we still are not finished. It is very important to standardize the solution to prevent recurrence. This crucial step prevents the common phenomenon of solving the same problem over and over again. Documenting proper work procedures, often with flowcharts, and training the employees in use of these procedures, are helpful in standardization. For example, if Acme had not instituted a procedure for routine measurement of flushability and for proper application of X-Pro, the same problem could have occurred again in a couple of years and gone undetected for some time. Without formal standardization, the gradual turnover of people knowledgeable about the problem frequently leads to recurrence.

THE PROBLEM SOLVING STRATEGY
AND THE STATISTICAL THINKING MODEL

The Problem Solving Strategy, like the Process Improvement Strategy, should be viewed as a more specific and detailed example of the Statistical Thinking Model in Figure 7.1. When we initiate the Problem Solving Strategy, we have already obtained data that indicate the presence of special causes. The *Document the Problem* step organizes the analysis of these data to enable easier diagnosis of the root cause. We use the data and analysis to update Subject Matter Theory with the *Identify Potential Root Causes* and *Choose Best Solutions* steps.

We begin the cycle again when we plan our solutions in the *Implement/Test Solutions* phase. The *Measure Results* step provides the actual data and analysis to determine whether the problem has been solved, and whether we need to loop back to identify and test other potential solutions. This completes the cycle back to updating our subject matter knowledge. The knowledge gained about the process is a fringe benefit of the Problem Solving Strategy (in addition to solving the problem). This can prove valuable in uses of the Process Improvement or Problem Solving Strategies, as well as during routine operation of the process.

The *Standardize* step involves ensuring that the original root cause does not recur. This may require some clarification or addition to the flowchart of the process, as depicted at the top of Figure 7.1. These changes will generally not be fundamental changes to the process, since the special causes that led to the problem are not, by definition, a fundamental part of the process.

As with the Process Improvement Strategy, the Problem Solving Strategy incorporates the key elements of the Statistical Thinking approach.

- Improving results by improving the process
- Diagnosing and reducing variation
- Synergy between subject matter theory and data
- A sequential approach

ENDNOTES

1. This case study is courtesy of Roger Hoerl.
2. Readers familiar with designed experiments will recognize this is a 2^{3-1} fractional factorial. While there are more risks with this design than with many others, each condition required two days to prepare and run, and the team felt that this design was better than no design at all.

The Realized Revenue Fiasco

10

The following case study involves structural variation in a business process. The participants began following the Process Improvement Strategy, came upon a special cause, and moved to the Problem Solving Strategy. While investigating the special cause, they discovered it to be a repeatable, predictable part of the system and successfully implemented a common cause solution. In general, when faced with structural variation, we should try to eliminate it using the Problem Solving Strategy. In some cases however, such as seasonal variation in the sales of cross-country skis, this will not be possible. If removing the structure is not an option, return to the Process Improvement Strategy to mitigate the effects of the structural variation.

CASE STUDY: THE REALIZED REVENUE FIASCO[1]

Connie, the marketing manager for At-Care Brand surgical supplies, was in hot water. Her December net realized revenue had come in well below budget, throwing off her fourth quarter results. The numbers were so bad that they caused the entire Health Care Division of Atlas Industries to miss its budget for the year. Worst of all, her boss, the vice president of the Health Care Division, had lost his annual bonus as a result. Connie was given very clear direction that this type of miss could never occur again.

She called in a statistical consultant to develop a realized revenue forecasting model to avoid future surprises. They began a discussion of how realized revenue is calculated, which led to the

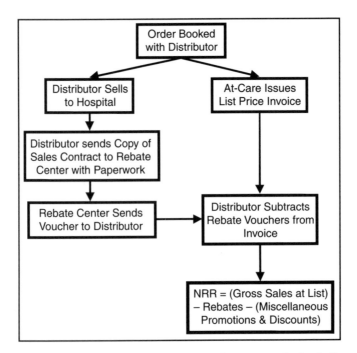

Figure 10.1 Flowchart of Net Realized Revenue Calculation.

flowchart in Figure 10.1. At-Care products were sold to large distributors, rather than directly to hospitals. To hide its pricing policies from competition, as well as to maximize profit, At-Care's list prices were rather high. Although virtually all sales were originally booked at full list price, At-Care offered distributors a number of discounts through a complicated rebate system. This approach enabled At-Care to sell to major final customers at competitive prices (after rebate), while obtaining high margins from smaller customers, or one-time buyers. The discounts were provided to distributors in the form of vouchers, which could be deducted from their next invoice.

When asked for data, Connie supplied detailed monthly information on sales for the year, price discounts given directly to the distributor, and each specific type of rebate. This information was broken down by customer, distributor, sales territory, sales region, and several product groupings. In fact, most people were intimidated by all the data and only looked at net realized revenue, the

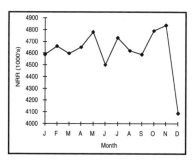

Figure 10.2   Time Plot of Realized Revenue.

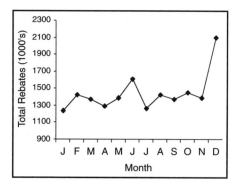

Figure 10.3   Time Plot of Total Rebates.

bottom line. Due to the panic over missing fourth quarter earnings, the data had been researched sufficiently to suggest that unusually high December rebates were the primary cause of low net realized revenue. Surprisingly, none of these data had been plotted.

A run chart of net realized revenue for the year (Figure 10.2) shows an obvious special cause in December. In discussing potential root causes, Connie pointed to December rebates, which were higher than she could remember. A run chart of total rebates (Figure 10.3) confirmed that December was also a special cause month for rebates. Asked "Why?" again, she said that she did not believe this was a seasonal effect, since distributors would naturally want their rebates as soon as possible.

Stratification analysis showed that December rebates were high across virtually all customers, distributors, sales regions, and

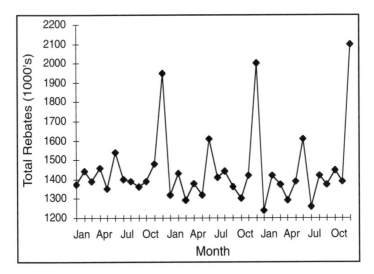

Figure 10.4 Three Years of Total Rebates.

product lines. *This ruled out many potential root causes. In addition, rebates were believed to lag the original sales by one to three months, due to the flow of paperwork. Connie hoped that a statistical forecasting model could be developed to model the lags and forecast rebates based on recent sales figures. Several time series models were attempted, but none provided any useful degree of prediction.*

At this point, it was back to the drawing board to take another look at the data. The more extensive historical files used in the attempt at time series modeling showed some interesting behavior. Figure 10.4 shows a run chart of rebates for the past three years. Structural variation was immediately apparent, with large peaks every December and smaller peaks each June.

Connie was shocked to see this plot, because she did not remember low net realized revenue in previous Decembers, and her beliefs were confirmed by the plot in Figure 10.5. In contemplating the reasons, she asked to see gross sales data, plotted in Figure 10.6. This showed that unusually high December sales the previous two years had masked high rebates, resulting in an apparently typical month.

The reasons were clear to Connie. The sales force had been asked to "peak" or "load" during the last two Decembers, a com-

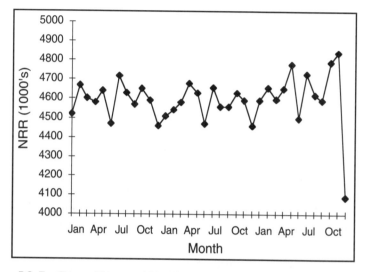

Figure 10.5 Three Years of Net Realized Revenue.

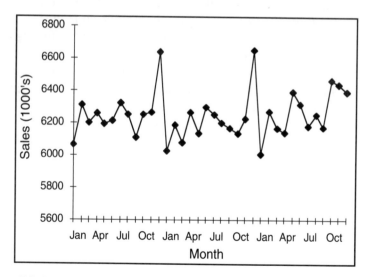

Figure 10.6 Three Years of Gross Sales.

mon practice when a business wants to boost its sales figures at the end of the year (often at the expense of sales in January). Customers are enticed to buy in December with incentives such as significantly discounted pricing, extended billing terms (so the customer does not pay until they use the product), and offers to carry the inventory costs of the product until the customer actually needs it. When asked about the most recent December, she said that they were doing well versus budget and did not feel the need to peak to achieve their annual goals. She realized that peaking incurred significant costs elsewhere in the system, and was concerned that if she exceeded budget by too large a margin, her budget would be set much higher next year.

Peaking explained why high rebates had gone undetected in previous Decembers, but did not explain their existence. Scatter plots of December rebates versus previous months' sales, as well as more sophisticated modeling techniques, had failed to provide any clue. They needed more information, so Connie and the consultant drove about 20 miles and visited the rebate center to talk to the people actually handling rebates and vouchers.

At the rebate center, they reviewed the process in greater detail with the people who actually worked in it. These people acknowledged a significant increase in voucher requests in late November. It appeared that distributors frequently waited until the end of the year to complete paperwork for sales contracts accumulated over several months. The paperwork was submitted with just enough time to receive the vouchers and deduct them from their last bills of the year. In other words, December was not as bad as it looked, but rebates for previous months should have been higher.

Connie still was surprised that distributors would not be more prompt in obtaining their vouchers. Follow-up calls to key distributors revealed that they were too understaffed to stay on top of the paperwork. Even though it delayed their rebates, they often put off completing the necessary paperwork until year end, or mid-year if they were on a fiscal versus calendar year. Distributors on a July-June fiscal year explained the smaller increase in rebates in June.

Connie realized that this was a predictable special cause—one that could be expected every December until the process was changed. On page 34, we referred to this as structural variation. Since structural variation is really inherent to the process, improvement requires fundamental change to the process, in this case, the rebate system.

While peaking could partially offset high rebates, it is an expensive business practice. It often hurts future sales at least as much as it helps December sales, and requires significant give-aways to entice customers to buy in December. Connie decided to completely replace the information system with one that would allow electronic billing and payment, and more importantly, automatically determine any rebate, subtract it from the next invoice to the distributor, and deduct it from the current month's net realized revenue. This solution is similar to what is commonly called reengineering, an improvement activity that attempts to wipe the slate clean and totally redesign a process from scratch, often utilizing state-of-the-art information technology.

Follow-up with Connie about 18 months later indicated that the new information system had resolved the problem of high June and December rebates, and also provided benefits in other areas.

Several important points are worth repeating relative to this case study:

- A great deal of pertinent information was available, but not used. In particular, nobody plotted the data. The root cause was easy to diagnose with simple plots, which made sophisticated modeling, Connie's original request, unnecessary. This confirmed the old saying (attributed to Yogi Berra) that "You can see a lot just by looking."

- Applying statistical methods without the process context of Statistical Thinking is often fruitless. The consultant's sophisticated time series models showed nothing, and the idea was rendered obsolete once the process view was taken.

- The problem went undiagnosed for years because of the lack of a process view. Until the December fiasco, people only looked at the key output, net realized revenue, and ignored indicators of the health of the process, such as sales, margins, and rebates. While improved process outputs are our objective, we need to carefully manage the process to achieve these outputs.

- Managing to budget is often inconsistent with the concept of continuous improvement. In this case, the budget was a restraint preventing people from achieving even better results. Improvement opportunities were overlooked as long as it appeared the budget would be achieved.

- When looking at monthly data, it is usually helpful to plot over several years to diagnose potential seasonality. The obvious seasonal pattern in rebates was missed because only the current year's data were plotted.
- To understand finer details of a business process, it is often very helpful to talk with people who actually work in the process on a daily basis.

The case study is a good demonstration of the Process Improvement and the Problem Solving Strategies in light of structural variation. While the case study doesn't follow the steps exactly as they are described in Chapter 8 and Chapter 9, it is a good demonstration of how they can be adapted during an improvement project.

Connie and the consultant began the process improvement strategy by describing the problem with a flowchart and collecting data on an important process measure, net realized revenue. It became clear that the process was not stable—December was the result of a special cause. They entered the Problem Solving Strategy and began to document the problem with sales and rebate data. Further discussions led to the root cause, which was related to large rebate volumes and the fact that the sales force didn't peak their sales in the most recent December.

Since the rebates were predictably high every December, they were really part of the process, in other words, structural variation, which meant a return to the Process Improvement Strategy. Process capability and common cause variation weren't major issues here, but when they began to study cause-and-effect relationships, they discovered a process so complex that At-Care's distributors didn't have time to complete the paperwork. Connie ultimately planned and implemented a system change by re-engineering the process and replacing the information system.

FINANCIAL IMPLICATIONS

An important part of understanding business processes is understanding the financial implications of the status quo. Financial experts sympathetic to Statistical Thinking can be quite helpful. Questions such as the following should be answered at the beginning of a process improvement effort to assure that it will return value to the organization.

- What are the financial consequences of continuing to perform as in the past?
- What is the cost of the present operation relative to what the cost would be if everything went right?
- What is the stated cost of scrap and rework, including repeat customer contacts because your customer service was not right the first time?
- Is that cost valued only at the price of raw materials, or does it take into account the fixed and variable costs (including time) up to the point of disaster?
- Is the cost of lost opportunity also factored in?
- What is the cost, due to low morale, of having to destroy or rework partially manufactured product or having to win back lost customers due to poor service?

Answers to these and similar questions will help assure that your strategy is right for your organization.

ENDNOTE

1. This case study comes from Hoerl and Snee (2000). *Statistical Thinking for Business Improvement.*

Tools Used in Statistical Thinking ◁ 11

The Process Improvement Strategy (Figure 8.8) and the Problem Solving Strategy (Figure 9.5) include a variety of tools typically used in Statistical Thinking applications. To effectively employ the strategies, practitioners need to develop competency to apply the tools themselves. Excellent materials have already been published about many of these tools, and for the most part, we have chosen to reference these materials instead of providing detailed descriptions here. Exceptions are affinity diagrams and interrelationship digraphs, which are discussed in Chapter 13 and some commentary on control charts later in this chapter. The primary companion reference we suggest is *The Memory Jogger II*, by Brassard and Ritter, published by GOAL/QPC. This book provides real examples and step by step instructions for applying many of the tools from the two strategies (see Table 11.1).

STATISTICAL THINKING TOOLS NOT IN *THE MEMORY JOGGER II*

The two strategies also use tools that are not covered in *The Memory Jogger II*. These are listed in Table 11.2 and are the focus of the remainder of this chapter. We'll provide descriptions of the Five Whys, data sheets, disaggregation, Is/Is Not analysis, and stratification. The remaining tools are extensive fields in their own rights and could not possibly be done justice in this book. We provide brief commentaries on these topics and refer interested

Table 11.1 Statistical Thinking Tools Discussed in *The Memory Jogger II.*

- Affinity Diagram
- Brainstorming
- Cause and Effect Diagram (Fishbone)
- Check Sheet
- Control Charts
- Flowcharts
- Histograms
- Interrelationship Digraph
- Multi-voting (also called Nominal Group Technique)
- Pareto Chart
- Run Chart
- Scatter Plot

Table 11.2 Process Improvement and Problem Solving Strategy Tools Not Discussed in *The Memory Jogger II.*

- "5 Whys"
- Data Sheets
- Disaggregation
- Experimental Design
- Model Building
- Procedures

readers to the following books for more information (see references for full publication information):

- *Statistics for Experimenters,* by Box, Hunter, and Hunter, for experimental design and model building.
- *Kaizen,* by Imai, for procedures and standards.
- *Making Instruction Work,* by Mager, for training.
- *What is a Survey?* published by American Statistical Association (ASA) Section on Survey Methodology, for surveys. See the ASA's Survey Research Section website at *www.stat.ncsu.edu/info/srms/survwhat.html* for more information.

- *Statistical Intervals: A Guide for Practitioners,* by Hahn and Meeker, for statistical inference.

We conclude the chapter with a discussion of control charting. While control charting is included in *The Memory Jogger II,* recent statistical literature has created much confusion about when, how, and why control charts can (and can't) be applied. We would like to reiterate the original concepts of control charting to provide some clarification for practitioners.

Five Whys

The *Five Whys* is a technique used to get from symptoms to root cause. As a rule of thumb, we may have to ask the question, Why?, five times before we reach the root cause. For example, suppose we are investigating the cause of a hospital employee being injured at work.

1. Why was Diane injured? She slipped and broke her hip.
2. Why did she slip? She stepped into a puddle of water on the floor.
3. Why was a puddle of water on the floor? The water fountain was leaking.
4. Why was the water fountain leaking? We canceled our maintenance contract.
5. Why did we cancel our maintenance contract?

The answer to the fifth Why is much more likely to reveal the root cause of the accident, rather than the fact that Diane slipped in a puddle of water. Stopping at question two might lead to simply mopping up the puddle, which would not prevent recurrence. Similarly, declining market shares, increased logistics costs, or declining price realization are symptoms, rather than root causes of poor business results.

Data Sheets

Data sheets are essentially check sheets used for gathering continuous (variables) data. (Check sheets are typically used for discrete or attribute data.) Everyone collecting the data should have a common understanding about how the data will be collected and the number of decimal places to report. When designing a data sheet, keep in mind how the data will be collected and used. For example, if the data will be entered into a computer spread-sheet, it helps to use the same columns on the paper that will be used in the spreadsheet.

Disaggregation

Disaggregation involves studying sub-processes. It is a useful common-cause strategy for processes that can be measured at several steps. The goal can be to identify the process step that takes the longest, the step with the most variation, or the step that is the largest bottleneck or constraint to the process.

The most common applications are measurements of the time required to perform a task. Examples include the time to process a loan application, to receive medical laboratory results, or to change from one product to another in a factory. Many tasks are required to complete these processes, and the amount of time taken can be measured for each task.

Is/Is Not Analysis

Is/Is Not analysis, attributed to Kepner-Tregoe (1979), is a method for rigorously documenting a problem. This documentation is extremely valuable when developing and evaluating ideas about the root cause of the problem. It is fairly common to document when, where, and what, and if appropriate, with whom a problem is associated, as in "problems with excessive heat began on line one at about ten o'clock last night."

What is not typically documented is where (what, when, who) we are NOT having a problem, but could. In the above example, suppose we documented that lines two and three had no prob-lems, but could have. Similarly, there were no problems prior to 10:00, and no other problems typically associated with excessive heat. This information is very helpful in brainstorming and eval-uating possible root causes. By explicitly stating where (what, when, who) the problem is not taking place, we can begin nar-rowing our search. In this case, what is different about line one, where the problem occurred, versus lines two and three? What could have occurred around 10:00, but not prior to then? What causes could explain the presence of excessive heat, but not

	IS	IS NOT	Potential Explanations	Actions
Where	Northeast	South, Midwest, Northwest, or West	Different warehouses	Review data on individual warehouses
What	Out of stock on many parts	Late delivery	Delivery process OK, but not inventory management	Check inventory management system
When	Begun around beginning of October	Prior to that time	New computer system Sept. 30; inventory reduction efforts began in October	Check differences in inventory mgt. algorithms; document changes in inventory targets
Who	All order takers	NA	NA	NA

Figure 11.1   Is/Is Not Analysis for Problems Supplying Customers in a Timely Fashion in Distribution.

other problems typically seen with excessive heat? This would typically be laid out in a spreadsheet, as in Figure 11.1, from Hoerl & Snee (2000), which addresses the problem of inability to supply customers in a timely fashion.

Stratification

Stratification is nothing more than breaking the data into logical categories to detect and isolate differences. In a manufacturing setting, we may wish to stratify by shift, by product line, by plant, and so on. The resin variation reduction team stratified output by lot and discovered important lot-to-lot variation. In a credit department, we might want to stratify by size of credit application (small versus jumbo), by branch office, or by individual worker.

While the overall system is of utmost importance, stratification helps us focus on root causes and find differences where we didn't expect them. Many statistical tools, such as histograms and scatter plots, can benefit from stratification. For example, when plotting the percent of defaulted loans versus loan amounts, a labeled scatter plot, with different symbols for each branch office, could reveal branch-to-branch differences, as well as the relationship, if any, between loan amount and defaults.

Experimental Design

Experimental design is unique among statistical methodologies in that it is completely proactive. Rather than analyzing existing data, we carefully plan which specific data would be most helpful in addressing the issue or problem. The effect of variation from sources outside our scope, such as different raw material lots, operating shifts, or locations, can be minimized by planning the data-collection process ahead of time. While passive monitoring of a process allows us to learn from informative events that happen to occur, experimental design actually creates the informative events from which to learn. By consciously inducing special causes into the process, we can significantly increase the speed with which we understand the relationships between the variables of interest. This approach is the best-known way of learning about variable relationships.

Model Building

Model building is a general term referring to the development of equations to quantify or predict process behavior. Typically, process outputs are modeled as a function of process variables or inputs. An accurate model allows us to predict, as well as understand how to intervene in the process to improve the outputs. Some models are based solely on subject matter theory, and are referred to as deterministic, or mechanistic, since they describe the fundamental, underlying mechanisms at work. These models are particularly common in physical sciences, where a great deal of exact, quantifiable theory exists, for example, $E = MC^2$. Other models use data to fit empirical equations, which can be thought of as approximations to the exact (but unknown) theoretical relationships. These models are used when it is not feasible to develop an exact theoretical model or where an approximation will suffice. Most models used in statistics are empirical models, often developed with data from designed experiments. The best practical approach, of course, is to combine subject matter knowledge with additional information contained in data.

Procedures

Procedures are agreed-upon, standardized, documented ways of doing work. A recipe is an everyday example of a procedure. Instructions for assembling a new bicycle or toy are other examples. Procedures add value by minimizing variation. If everyone follows the same procedure in doing the work, a large source of variation is eliminated. Procedures should also help all workers come closer to the level of the best worker. Procedures are typically the best way to maintain improvements gained through application of the Process Improvement Strategy. For the procedures to actually work and be used, it is critical that those actually doing the work are involved in their creation and upkeep. The procedure system must be maintained and upgraded as new and better ways of doing the work are developed. This prevents the procedures from becoming a bureaucracy.

Standards

As used here, *standards* are agreed-upon objectives for the outputs (or inputs) of the process. Typically these are in the form of specifications and targets. In some cases, they may be physical standards that define what a product should look or feel like. In service applications, they may be defined in terms of customer satisfaction. However they are defined, it is important to have clearly stated objectives or standards. If standards do not exist, then by definition everything is acceptable. Process capability is determined by comparing process variation to standards.

Statistical Inference

Statistical inference is the process of using data from a sample to draw conclusions about the process or population that provided the sample. For example, pollsters draw inferences about how the U.S. population will vote using data from a sample of several hundred people. A key conceptual issue in inference is determining how broadly we can extrapolate from our sample. For example, suppose we evaluate a new drug in an experimental study, using a sample of middle-aged women from Florida. If the drug works well in the study, can we conclude that it works for anyone, or only middle-aged women from Florida? Perhaps it works for all women, or all middle-aged women. The answer depends on the type of drug studied, and to what degree its success depends on the attributes of this particular sample. Note that our ability to extrapolate depends on subject-matter knowledge more than statistics. Statistics can quantify the uncertainty in the sample data, but it cannot quantify the degree to which it makes sense to extrapolate the results of the study.

Surveys

Surveys gather data from people. Many hotels, restaurants, and other service businesses use surveys regularly to gather information about customer satisfaction, or to determine customer preferences. Surveys are also helpful in obtaining input from a wide variety of people for an improvement project. Survey methodology is an extensive science, however. There are many pitfalls to avoid to ensure valid and meaningful data. Examples include non-response bias, leading questions, confusing questions, biased sampling (sampling only one political party on a political survey, for example), or lengthy surveys that deter people from completing them, leading to non-response bias. Non-response bias occurs when people do not respond to the survey, and these people differ in some important way from those who did respond. It is well known by psychologists, for example, that people who like to fill out surveys tend to have different personality types than those who don't.

Training

Training is the process of developing a person's competency to perform a specific task. It differs from education in that education develops general understanding of a subject. Lack of proper training is one of the most significant root causes of poor performance in virtually all human endeavors. There is an old saying, "Training is expensive. Good training is very expensive. No training is most expensive." As with procedures, training is a very important part of maintaining the gains from application of the Process Improvement Strategy. In fact, training and procedures go hand in hand, in that the procedures provide the content for the training, and training provides the vehicle to develop broad capability to apply the procedures. Since training develops competency to perform specific tasks, it is very important that careful thought go into defining the specific tasks trainees need to master. These skills should also be audited, at least at the end of the training, if not periodically from then on.

COMMENTS ON CONTROL CHARTS

The details of developing and using control charts are provided in *The Memory Jogger II*. This discussion is intended to clarify the purpose and broad applicability of control charts.

Many recent publications in statistical journals have misunderstood Shewhart's (1931) and (1939) original purpose for control charts and suggested that their use should be restricted to situations that satisfy narrow statistical criteria. For example, control charts have been portrayed as hypothesis tests about average or variation, simplistic time series models, or tools for on-line process adjustment (engineering control). It has even been suggested that control charts should not be used unless the data are exactly normally distributed, the process is already in a state of statistical control, and the data show no evidence of autocorrelation (correlation of successive observations).

Few, if any, of the multitude of successful applications of control charts (including those published by Shewhart himself) would meet these narrow statistical criteria. Certainly, there are situations where control charts are not the appropriate tool, but not for these reasons! See Wheeler and Chambers (1992) for further discussion of these misconceptions.

The real purpose of control charts is to differentiate between special and common causes of variation. Since control charts are not rigorous statistical hypothesis tests, narrow assumptions about the data or the process itself are unnecessary. The limits on the charts are intended as benchmarks or general guidelines for when to suspect special causes, not as rigid, legalistic criteria, as with a formal hypothesis test.

Control charts have two primary uses: as a diagnostic tool to study and learn about a process, and as a tool to monitor a process. Many times the first step in improvement is to study and understand the current process. The data for diagnostic control charting are collected, sometimes off-line, by a process improvement team. The initial data collection often raises questions that require additional data to identify sources of variation.

The more commonly touted use of control charts is process monitoring, where the purpose is to maintain a process in control. The data are usually collected by operational people, and corrective action is taken in real time. A process must be well diagnosed before control charts are effective for monitoring. Using control charts for monitoring poorly understood processes generally leads to frustration and resentment, particularly if there is no support for acting on the process when it is out of control but still meets standards.

In either mode, control charting is intended to be proactive, where we intervene to improve the process based on the information gleaned from the charts. Since Shewhart control charts provide graphs of the data themselves, they are excellent tools for developing theories, not just for testing them. We often see unexpected trends or patterns, leading us to ask questions, investigate, and revise our understanding of the process. This enables us to intervene appropriately, rather than tampering with the process in ignorance. The objective of control charting is to reduce variation, not just to model it.

A key success factor with control charts is the method of subgrouping the data. This is because the width of the chart limits is based on the variation within subgroups, which in turn is intended to represent common cause variation. The limits represent a "yardstick" for the amount of variation we would expect in subgroup averages if there were no variation between subgroups. Thus, it is important that within-subgroup variation reflects process variation that would normally occur between subgroups. Failure to use good subgrouping principles will result in control limits that are too narrow or too wide. For example, variation is likely to be small among samples within a subgroup if they are collected over an extremely small time frame. If, however, very long periods of time pass between subgroups, the variation between subgroups may be much larger than the within-subgroup variation. The result will be limits that are too narrow to function as a good yardstick for common cause variation. On the other hand, if structural variation is present within subgroups, the limits will be too wide. See Wheeler and Chambers (1992) for more information.

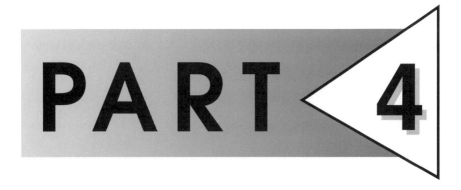

PART 4

IMPLEMENTING STATISTICAL THINKING CAPABILITY

Organizational Tips 12

It has been said that the half-life of a short course is four hours, and since most short courses end on a Friday, the likelihood of their application the following Monday is small indeed. The same might be said of all things read, including everything you've encountered so far in this book. Many have found that, to learn something, they must actually do it. Further, the importance of learning cannot be overstated. As American philosopher Eric Hoffer (1973) put it, "In a time of drastic change it is the learners who inherit the future. The learned usually find themselves equipped to live in a world that no longer exists" (p. 32).

This section is intended to provide ideas about how to actually do Statistical Thinking, so people will learn it and use it to benefit the organizations they support. This collection of ideas is not wholly sufficient for developing Statistical Thinking capability in an organization. After all, organizations abound where, because of management attitudes, fearful organizational cultures, and other barriers, thinking—Statistical or otherwise—is not permitted. Most organizations are not complete wastelands of negative attitudes, however, and those eager to apply Statistical Thinking will usually find at least a small corner of fertile ground.

IDENTIFY PRIORITIES FOR STATISTICAL THINKING APPLICATIONS

✎ Participants in Statistical Thinking tutorial sessions often voice concerns about where to begin. Simply put, the first applications of Statistical Thinking should be to real, important problems within reach of the organization. Choose something that people believe to be a source of lost opportunity or a waste of time, human resources, or money. The problem should be one over which the organization has control, that is, responsibility for the issue in question should reside within the organization. Crossing lines of responsibility in such problem-solving efforts will lead to failure and a great reluctance to try such methods again. An initial success, on the other hand, can attract attention and create interest in applying the concepts elsewhere in the organization.

✎ TIP

Process Improvement Oriented Questions

For the processes to be identified

- What processes (activities) are you responsible for? Who owns these processes? Who are the team members? How well does the team work together?
- Which processes have the highest priority for improvement? How do you know? What data did you use?

For the processes to be improved

- How is the process performing?
- What are your process performance measures? Why? How is the quality of the measurement system?
- How good or bad is the current process performance? What are the improvement goals for the process?
- Do you know the sources of variation in the process? Can your data collection strategy separate the sources?
- Are any sources of variation supplier-dependent? If so, have you involved the suppliers in the improvement effort?

In addition, remember to emphasize the process-view component of Statistical Thinking when getting started. Problems often develop between the steps of the flowchart, so it is important that initial applications of Statistical Thinking span multiple process operations. Applying Statistical Thinking to too small a problem will have negligible or perhaps even a negative impact, due to sub-optimization or small success for much effort.

Further, it is best to position Statistical Thinking as a *how* as opposed to a *what*. That is, Statistical Thinking is a means to accomplishing an end. It is not something else to do. If you have not been in this position yourself, picture managers who have 18 tasks to accomplish before noon tomorrow. Do you really think you are going to persuade them to do another? Chances of success are much higher if, instead, Statistical Thinking is seen as a way to get the work done.

USE GROUP THINKING FOR IMPROVEMENT AND INNOVATION

Those with Total Quality Management experience know that "none of us is as smart as all of us." Groups have synergistic power; that is, their combined thinking is generally better than the additive thinking of their members. Some TQM failure, however, has occurred because managers formed groups without taking responsibility for training their members to function as a team. Group formation is not as simple as saying, "Here are your ears. Now you are a Mouseketeer!" It takes structure and practice to form an effective team.

Structure is key to team effectiveness, as is understood by anyone who has suffered through meetings dominated by those with the highest rank or loudest voice. To be effective teams should meet with ground rules well defined. A starting set of rules is:

- Follow the meeting agenda.
- Respect and listen to all participants.
- Be honest and open.
- Do not give speeches.
- Do not engage in side-bar conversations.

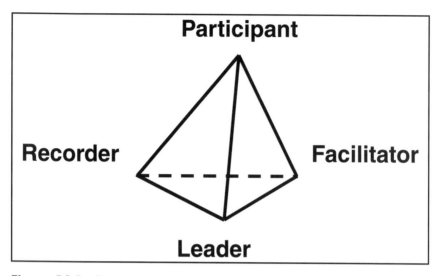

Figure 12.1 Team Composition.

Team leaders may want to ask participants to augment this list during initial meetings to accommodate any special operating circumstances. If nothing else, it encourages team buy-in to the rules.

A second form of structure is organizational. Doyle and Straus (1976) cite four key roles in team meetings (see Figure 12.1): team leader, facilitator, recorder, and participant. The **team leader** owns the problem and has responsibility for effecting the process improvement, solving the problem, or otherwise getting the job done. The leader takes responsibility for designing the meeting to produce the desired outcome by setting the stage to get the best thinking out of the team.

This is usually coordinated with the **facilitator,** who also serves as a neutral, third party during the meeting. The facilitator directs traffic, keeps the team on track with regard to the agenda, works to assure that all abide by the ground rules, tries to bring out the ideas of those who have not yet contributed, prevents personal attacks, and generally moderates the discussion. By doing these things, the facilitator frees the team leader to participate in the meeting.

Team memory is extremely important. Recall your misgivings after a meeting in which seemingly nothing was accomplished, nobody agreed about what was agreed upon, or the minutes (published a week or two later) disagreed with your recollections. In good meeting processes, the **recorder** records real-time, on flip charts, and in front of the whole team. The group memory is preserved immediately while the thoughts are fresh and while the opportunity for correction is ripe. This is an application of Statistical Thinking: It minimizes the variation in the record keeping process. The recorder must remain as neutral as the facilitator and must also check in with participants to assure that key thoughts are captured and summarized accurately.

A word about facilitator and recorder neutrality is in order here. Sometimes the urge for one of these people to participate becomes overwhelming. A key thought percolates to the surface and cannot be suppressed. Facilitators and recorders faced with this situation should announce that for the moment, they are stepping out of their role and into the role of the participant prior to offering their contributions.

In this setting, the **participant,** the most important element in the group process, has an opportunity to contribute on a level playing field. The participants' responsibility is to contribute their best thinking to solving the problem at hand. They also must follow the agenda and group process and work to assure that the facilitator and recorder stay in their roles.

Once ground rules are established and the team structure has been set, it remains for the team to practice working together. Performance will improve with practice, especially as members get to know each other better. Group cohesiveness exercises such as dinners and recreational events help.

EDUCATE RECOGNIZING A DIVERSITY
OF LEARNING STYLES

Professional educators say that people learn in different ways and that no single learning style is best for all. Effective lessons include elements that appeal to various styles of learning. Many education models exist, and as George Box (1979) has said about statistical models, "all models are wrong; some are useful." One useful model from McCarthy (1988) is "Feelings, Facts, Forms and Futures."

How does this apply to Statistical Thinking? If you are going to teach it, you will be wise to personalize it, provide the basic information, provide guided practice, and integrate it with the job function. This will appeal to the feelings, facts, forms, and futures thinkers, in that order.

Finally, understand that training is not a one-time event. Training is a process. It must be ongoing. How many managers trained everyone in Statistical Process Control but for some strange reason, it didn't take? In most cases there is little wonder. The applications were not present and immediate, and the training was a one-time shot with a four-hour half-life. Hoerl and Snee (1995) assert that training, and assessing the effectiveness of training, should be carried out using the principles of Statistical Thinking, much the same as in any other process.

For more information on the subject of training in Statistical Thinking, see the Special Publication *Statistical Thinking* published by the ASQ Statistics Division, as well as Britz, et al. (1997) and Hare, et al. (1995).

LEARNING STYLES: FEELINGS, FACTS, FORMS, AND FUTURES

People who are **Feelings** learners seek to understand *why* something should be done. Appealing to their emotions will frequently motivate them to learn. "This will serve the benefit of the organization; people will be happier; things will run more smoothly," for example. They are socially smart people who have interpersonal skills, and they learn best when things are personalized.

Facts learners are very logical. They want to know *what,* and learn by analyzing, reading texts and studying theories.

Those who want to know *how* are **Forms** learners. They learn by testing theories and are usually very detailed. Frequently they are the administrators.

Finally, **Futures** learners are the people who need to know *what if.* These intuitive thinkers learn by transfer of ideas from outside areas to their own areas.

No one is only one kind of learner. Everyone is some combination of these four types. This is why the best lessons, even those presented to very small homogeneous audiences, should contain elements that appeal to all four learning styles.

New Management Tools to Identify Implementation Barriers ◁ 13

Once a problem area has been identified, it is important to learn the reasons for its existence. TQM literature emphasizes "asking why" five times to get to root causes. Complex problems often exist for complex reasons, and getting to the root causes can take special tools. We present two of the most commonly used tools: the affinity diagram and the interrelationship digraph. As teams grow in ability and effectiveness, they can solve more complex problems and use more complex tools, such as the tree diagram and the prioritization matrix. These are described in *The Memory Jogger II*.

AFFINITY DIAGRAMS

Now that we can work as an effective team and have identified a problem whose solution is within our control, we must identify reasons for the problem's existence. Brainstorming, a tool that has been around since the 1920s, is effective at drawing out people's ideas, and affinity diagrams can effectively organize those ideas. The process is shown in Figure 13.1.

An affinity diagram works best in an environment that is free for honest expression of opinion, where ideas are considered rather than judged, and where group focus is maintained on the problem at hand. On one occasion, for example, group members were given the following:

Managers resist Statistical Thinking because _____.

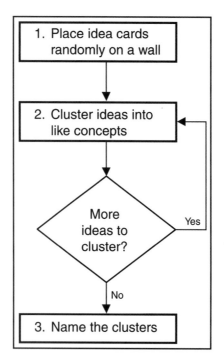

Figure 13.1 Affinity Diagram Process.

Participants were asked to fill in the blank with a phrase or complete sentence. (If phrases are used, a helpful guideline is that they contain a verb.) The question had been printed on individual Post-it® notes so, once completed, they could be stuck randomly to the wall. A small group of five to seven people then worked to form these ideas into clusters of like ideas.

There are special rules for this process. If you are right-handed, use your left hand for affinity mapping, and if you are left-handed, use the right. This practice is related to left-brain, right-brain theory and is supposed to help introduce a different set of neurons, a more spatially oriented set, to the solution of the problem. If you doubt this, then (1) you have company, and (2) you might recall the number of times you have left work with a problem you couldn't solve only to have a solution pop into your head while you were driving home. Driving is a spatial exercise, and the spatial side of your brain began to work on the problem that the analytical side of your brain did not solve.

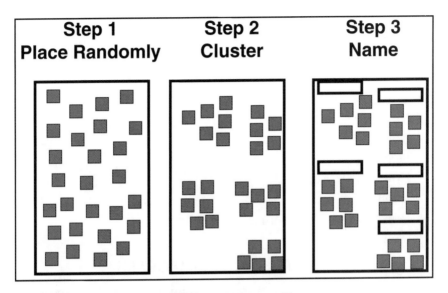

Figure 13.2   Summary of Affinity Diagram Steps.

Another affinity mapping rule is silence. The logic is the same: Talking is an analytical exercise, and you want to operate spatially. Talking would interfere with that operation and slow the process to a crawl.

The team should continue to move the notes into clusters until most of the activity ceases. A few orphan ideas may be left over. That is normal. It is also possible that one person will move a note into a cluster and someone else will move it to another. Kicking and biting is discouraged, but it is acceptable to move a note to another location after it has already been placed by someone else. When the exercise is over, the team members can discuss reasons for the difference of opinion. Usually they are associated with differing interpretations of the content of the note.

Next, the team should work together, talking now permitted, to name the clusters. Names should be as short and distinctive as possible while, at the same time, representative and comprehensive of the ideas in the cluster. Orphan ideas can be named or ignored, depending on how important the team believes they are. Often orphans are so classified because they lack relevance. A sketch of the steps of creating an affinity diagram is presented in Figure 13.2.

The team that worked on management acceptance of Statistical Thinking clustered approximately 80 ideas into eight barriers, including:

- Lack of training
- Threat to authority
- Not a business method
- Don't understand it
- Fear of statistics
- Unwilling to change
- Too busy
- Don't want to be confused by the facts

INTERRELATIONSHIP DIGRAPH

Clearly, the affinity diagram helped by narrowing the number of reasons from approximately 80 down to a more workable eight. Still, the solution is not clear. If the team wanted managers to accept Statistical Thinking, what would they do? Would they tackle all eight major barriers simultaneously? The interrelationship digraph, or ID, complements an affinity diagram and helps answer these questions. The primary purpose of an ID is to sort major causes into drivers and effects.

A flowchart of the ID process is in Figure 13.3. To learn which reason drives the problem or is most important in its solution, set the header cards (containing the cluster names from the affinity diagram) in a circle. The facilitator starts with the card at the top of the circle and compares it with every other card, asking

1. Does the top card cause the other card, or
2. Does the other card cause the top card, or
3. Is there no relationship?

The facilitator seeks team consensus on these answers. If that does not happen, a separate discussion of the issue must take place. Often, differences are due to variation in interpretation. When consensus is reached, the facilitator draws an arrow from the card that caused the effect to the other card, unless of

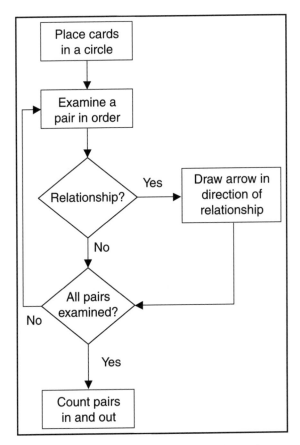

Figure 13.3   Flowchart of Interrelationship Digraph.

course, there is no relationship. Note that no double-headed arrows are permitted.

When all relationships involving the top card have been decided, the facilitator should use the next card in the clockwise direction as the starting position and examine relationships between it and all remaining cards. Then the facilitator should move to the card after that in the clockwise direction, and so on until all relationships have been established.

The next step is to visit each card, counting arrows in and arrows out. The cards with the most arrows out are the drivers;

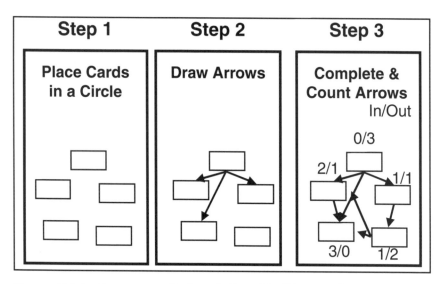

Figure 13.4 Summary of Interrelationahip Digraph Steps.

the remaining cards are the effects. Usually there are only two or three drivers. Accuracy can be checked by verifying that the number of arrows in is equal to the number of arrows out. A summary of the steps of an ID is displayed in Figure 13.4

A small group used an ID on our example. Here's what they came up with:

	Arrows In	Arrows Out
Lack of training	2	4
Threat to authority	3	1
Not a business method	3	0
Don't understand it	2	4
Fear of statistics	1	4
Unwilling to change	2	2
Too busy	0	2
Don't want to be confused by the facts	4	0
Total	17	17

There are three key barriers to the use of Statistical Thinking, each with four arrows coming out of their boxes:

- Managers lack training.
- Managers don't understand it.
- Managers fear statistics.

What can be done about them? Institute training as a first step, but be careful how you do it! (Remember the material presented on page 134.) Training is a process like any other business process. It should not be treated as a one-time event. The principles of Statistical Thinking apply to training as they do for all processes. The training must be followed by practice and experience, perhaps with the help of a Statistical Thinking mentor.

Practice Scenarios

14

You can use the following four scenarios as you educate people and apply Statistical Thinking in your operation. Of course, there are no right or wrong answers to the questions; instead they should be offered to generate discussion and learning. Discussion of two scenarios ("Right Illness, Wrong Prescription" and "Sales Rep of the Year") has been published in *Quality Progress* (Britz, et al. 1997).

WHERE'S THE BEEF?

On March 5, 1996, USA TODAY *reported "Beef Industry Hits Hard Times—Experts Say Answer Rests in Satisfying Customers." The $37 billion beef industry is losing market share to chicken and pork: 34 percent share in 1996 down from a 52 percent share in 1976. Annual beef consumption has decreased from 85 lb./person in 1970 to 67 lb./person in 1996, while annual poultry consumption has increased from 41 to 72 lb./person during the same time period.*

The problem is inconsistent product. "I can go into a store now and look through 20 steaks to find one that's acceptable. But a chicken breast is a chicken breast," says one consumer. The poultry industry has changed how its products are raised, prepared, packaged, and marketed. According to a 1991 study, consumers are not satisfied one in five times they cook or order beef. Complaints ranged from confusion over various grades of beef to difficulty cooking, to toughness or unpleasant beef.

*And, in an era of increasing emphasis on healthy diets, con-
sumers say they now avoid red meat because its fat and cholesterol
content makes it a less healthy choice.*

Questions:

Assuming these comments are representative of many customers' feelings,

a) Can the use of Statistical Thinking help solve this problem?
    Why or why not?
b) If so, how should the beef industry respond, using
    Statistical Thinking?

GOLDEN ACRES

*Nurse's aide Kari Taker was talking to Arthur Ritus, one of her col-
leagues at the Golden Acres Health Care Center.*

*"Why must we remove the seat belt from Helen Wheeler's
wheelchair? You know what'll happen when she tries to stand up.
She'll fall flat on her face."*

*Art replied, "It'll be okay. We have those new movement moni-
tors to alert us if she tries to stand up."*

*"But Art, you know how impulsive Helen is. She'll try to stand
up before anyone can get over to help her. Who came up with this
dumb rule any way?"*

*"Kari, you know that this is a federal mandate. It says and I
quote: 'The resident has the right to be free from any physical or
chemical restraints imposed for purposes of discipline or conve-
nience, and not required to treat the resident's medical symptoms.'
I'm sure there have been abuses that led to writing this mandate.
I've read of studies that show the bad things that can happen to people who are over-medicated and/or restrained."*

*"Yes, but I wonder if there are any studies that document what
happens to people who are not properly medicated and/or are not
restrained. You know as well as I do Art, that the definitions and
guidelines are rather vague, and there is no specific list of medical
symptoms. Yet states are told that they will not receive federal
money if they don't abide by the mandate."*

"Yes, and now states are auditing the health care centers. Last week we had two auditors in our building, and you know what? Each auditor is interpreting the mandate differently. And, of course, we're threatened with loss of funding if our facility doesn't comply."

"Well Art, I guess we just have to go along with it. I hope Helen doesn't get hurt because of the residents' so-called rights."

Three days passed.

"Kari, whose monitor is going off?"

"Oh no, it's Helen's! She's already fallen! I hope she's not badly hurt. What a price to pay for her rights!"

Questions:

a) How could government agencies have used Statistical Thinking to prevent this situation?

b) How can nursing homes use Statistical Thinking to address the current problem?

RIGHT ILLNESS, WRONG PRESCRIPTION

Benjamin Dover had just completed an intensive course in Statistical Thinking for Continuous Improvement, which was offered to all employees of a large health maintenance organization (HMO). There was no time to celebrate, however, because he was already under a lot of pressure. Ben worked as a pharmacist's assistant in the HMO's pharmacy, and his manager, Juan de Pacotilla, was about to be fired because of numerous complaints, and even a few lawsuits, over inaccurate prescriptions. Juan now was asking Ben for his assistance in trying to resolve the problem, preferably yesterday!

"Ben, I really need your help! If I can't show some major improvement, or at least a solid plan, by next month, I'm history."

"I'll be glad to help, Juan, but what can I do, I'm just a pharmacist's assistant."

"I don't care what your job title is. I think you're just the person who can get this done. I've been too far removed from day-to-day

operations in the pharmacy, but you work there every day. You're in a much better position to find out how to fix the problem. Just tell me what to do, and I'll do it."

"But what about the statistical consultant you hired to analyze the data on inaccurate prescriptions."

"Ben, to be honest, I'm really disappointed with that guy. He has spent two weeks trying to come up with a new modeling approach to predict weekly inaccurate prescriptions. I tried to explain to him that I don't want to predict the mistakes, I want to eliminate them! I don't think I got through, though, because he said we need a month of additional data to verify the model before he can apply a new method. He just read about it in a journal, and it's supposed to identify 'change points in the time series,' whatever that means. But get this, he will only identify the change points and send me a list. He says it's my job to figure out what they mean, and how to respond! I don't know much about statistics—the only thing I remember from college is that it was the worst course I ever took—but I'm becoming convinced that it really doesn't have much to offer in solving real problems. You've just gone through this Statistical Thinking course though, so maybe you can see something I can't. To me Statistical Thinking sounds like an oxymoron! I realize it's a long shot, but I was hoping you could use this as the project you need to complete the course officially."

"I see your point, Juan, I felt the same way too. This course was interesting, though, because it didn't focus on crunching numbers. I have some ideas about how we can approach making improvements in prescription accuracy, and I think this would be a great project. We may not be able to solve it ourselves, though. As you know, there is a lot of finger-pointing. The pharmacists blame sloppy handwriting and incomplete instructions from doctors. Doctors blame pharmacy assistants, like me, who actually enter the prescriptions into the computer, claiming that we are incompetent. And the assistants tend to blame the pharmacists for assuming too much about our knowledge of medical terminology, brand names, known drug interactions, and so on."

"It sounds like there's no hope, Ben!"

"I wouldn't say that at all, Juan, it's just that there may be no quick fix we can do by ourselves just in the pharmacy. Let me *explain how I'm thinking about this, and how I would propose attacking the problem using what I just learned in the Statistical Thinking course."*

Question:

How do you think Ben should approach this problem, using what he has just learned?

SALES REP OF THE YEAR[1]

Ron Hagler, VP of Sales for Selit Corporation, wanted to see his regional sales managers right away. His staff assistant, Bonnie Teller, had just compiled the past five years of quarterly sales data for the regions under his authority. He was not happy with the results! "Marsha, Tell the regional managers I need to speak with them this afternoon. Everyone must attend. Oh, and get us a conference room."

Marsha Underwood had been Tom's secretary for almost a decade. She knew by the tone in his voice that he meant business. She immediately checked the availability of the isolated conference rooms until she found one. The meeting was set for 2:00. At 1:55, the regional managers filed into the room. The only time they were called into a meeting together was when Ron was not happy.

Ron wasted no time. "Bonnie just finished the fourth quarter sales report. New England sales were fantastic. Steve, you not only improved 17.6 percent over last quarter, but you also increased sales a whopping 20.6 percent over last year. I don't know how you do it!" Steve smiled. His philosophy was to end the year with a bang; to get the customers to stockpile units. First quarter sales were always sluggish, but a decline in sales at the beginning of the year always went unnoticed.

Ron continued. "Terry, Southwestern sales were also superb. You showed an 11.7 percent increase over last quarter and an 11.8 percent increase over last year." Terry also smiled. She wasn't sure how she had done so well, but she sure wasn't going to change anything.

"Jan, the Northwestern sales were up 17.2 percent from last quarter, but down 8.2 percent from last year. You need to find out what you did last year to make your sales go through the roof. Even so, your performance this quarter was good." Jan tried to hide his puzzled look. Sales for the Northwest were declining. In November, a new Smith Brothers store had opened. It was the first big order he had received in a long time.

Ron was now ready to deal with the problem regions. "Leslie, North Central sales were down 5.5 percent from last quarter, but up 4.7 percent from last year. I don't understand how your sales vary so much. Do you need more incentive?" Leslie looked down. She had been working very hard the past five years, and had acquired numerous new accounts—in fact, she had received a bonus the previous year for acquiring the most new business.

"Kim, the Mid-Atlantic sales were down 3.2 percent from last quarter and 2.6 percent from last year. I'm very disappointed in your performance. You were once my best sales rep. I had high expectations for you. Now, I can only hope that your first quarter results show some sign of life." Kim felt her face get red. She knew she had sold more units this year than in the previous year. . . What does Ron know anyway. He's just an empty suit.

As Ron turned to Dave, he felt a surge of adrenaline. "Dave, South Central sales are the worst of all! Sales are down 19.7 percent from last quarter and down 22.3 percent from last year. How can you explain this? Do you value your job? I want to see a dramatic improvement in this quarter's results or else!" Dave felt numb. This was a tough region, with a lot of competition. Sure, accounts were lost over the years, but those lost were always replaced with new ones. How could he be doing so badly?

Questions:

a) What assumptions is Ron making in his interpretation of the data? The data are on pages 149 and 150.

b) What questions should Ron ask?

c) What is the correct interpretation of the data?

Sales by Region 1991

Region	Q1	Q2	Q3	Q4
NE	924	928	956	1222
SW	1056	1048	1129	1073
NW	1412	1280	1129	1181
NC	431	470	439	431
MA	539	558	591	556
SC	397	391	414	407

Sales by Region 1992

Region	Q1	Q2	Q3	Q4
NE	748	962	983	1024
SW	1157	1146	1064	1213
NW	1149	1248	1103	1021
NC	471	496	506	573
MA	540	590	606	643
SC	415	442	384	448

Sales by Region 1993

Region	Q1	Q2	Q3	Q4
NE	991	978	1040	1295
SW	1088	1322	1256	1132
NW	1085	1125	910	999
NC	403	440	371	405
MA	657	602	596	640
SC	441	366	470	426

Sales by Region 1994

Region	Q1	Q2	Q3	Q4
NE	765	1008	1038	952
SW	1352	1353	1466	1196
NW	883	851	997	878
NC	466	536	551	670
MA	691	723	701	802
SC	445	455	363	462

Sales by Region 1995

Region	Q1	Q2	Q3	Q4
NE	1041	1020	976	1148
SW	1330	1003	1197	1337
NW	939	834	688	806
NC	588	699	743	702
MA	749	762	807	781
SC	420	454	447	359

ENDNOTE

1. The authors thank Don Wheeler for contributing this data set.

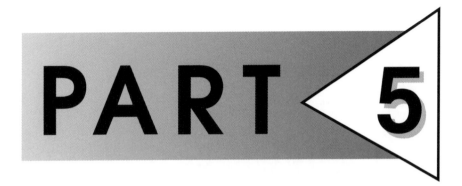

PART 5

SUMMARY

Summary

Here is a summary of the key ideas in the preceding chapters. As with all summaries, it is not adequate to cover the content entirely. The intent is to provide a reminder of the key points presented.

WHY IS STATISTICAL THINKING IMPORTANT?

As economies and organizations are globalized, as the globe shrinks and worldwide communications become commonplace, and as competition increases in ferocity, the need to operate efficiently is ever increasing. Statistical Thinking is an extremely effective and proven approach to achieving this efficient operation. Without it, process management is ineffective and improvement is slowed. With it, organizations prosper because learning takes place, and performance is improved.

WHAT IS STATISTICAL THINKING?

Statistical Thinking is a philosophy of learning and action based on the following fundamental principles:

- All work occurs in a system of interconnected processes.
- Variation exists in all processes.
- Understanding and reducing variation are keys to success.

Successful organizations learn and grow. Organizations that do not ultimately fail. Learning requires accumulation of information, usually by taking the right amount of the right kind of data to make decisions for improvement. Learning without action is wasteful and useless. However, learning, taking action toward gains, and holding those gains lead to organizational success and longevity.

This cannot be accomplished by perfecting individual unit operations. Instead, it requires a systemic view and examination of the process as a whole. It is only by viewing the work as a system of interconnected processes that true system understanding and improvement can occur.

It is important to understand that all processes naturally exhibit variation. The world is too complex to permit a deterministic view of all events. Chance variation happens everywhere. Variation hurts when a process is centered on the proper target but exhibits too much noise. It also hurts when a process is centered at an incorrect target. Losses increase, often exponentially, as variation from target increases.

We categorize variation as coming from common, special, and structural causes. The distinction is important to getting to the final point of the definition: Understanding and reducing variation are keys to success. These are not the only keys to success, but they are fundamental elements. Processes that operate with less variation run more smoothly and efficiently. One way to minimize variation is to eliminate special causes. Another is to redesign to reduce the common cause variation. There are others, too.

Learning, action based on learning, a process view, variation, and data are key concepts of Statistical Thinking.

Statistical Thinking sets the stage for the application of statistical methods. Statistical Thinking is conceptual, its applications are universal, and it is based on the acquisition of knowledge, therefore it leads the improvement effort. When Statistical Thinking is applied, there are greater and more appropriate uses of statistical methods.

Statistical Thinking takes on different appearances depending on the organizational level where it is applied. We distinguish among the strategic, the managerial, and the operational levels of an organization. At the strategic level, executives map core processes, and they understand the importance of communication throughout the organization. They know the role of data and they value experimentation. At the managerial level, systems are put in place to assure that the provisions of the strategic plans are followed. Barriers between functional groups are eliminated. People work toward identifying true root causes of problems without fear of retribution. At the operational level, workers understand the importance of reducing variation. Process control is found in all aspects of the operation—not just on the production floor.

HOW IS STATISTICAL THINKING APPLIED?

To apply the principles of Statistical Thinking, we begin with as much process and subject matter knowledge as possible. Then we develop a plan to gather data whose analysis will lead to improvement. This, in itself, is an iterative process. We proceed from data to analysis to plan to more data, and so on. All the while, process knowledge increases.

We discuss two improvement strategies: The Process Improvement Strategy is an overall improvement approach, and the Problem Solving Strategy addresses special cause and structural variation encountered while using the Process Improvement Strategy. These improvement processes are linked to the scientific method and the Plan-Do-Check-Act or CAP-Do Cycle attributed to Deming (1982) and Shewhart.

Steps in the Process Improvement Strategy are

1. Describe the process.
2. Collect data on key process and output measures.
3. Assess process stability.
4. Address special cause variation.
5. Evaluate process capability.
6. Analyze common cause variation.
7. Study cause-and-effect relationships.
8. Plan and implement changes.

Steps in the Problem Solving Strategy are

1. Document the problem.
2. Identify potential root causes.
3. Choose the best solutions.
4. Implement and test the solutions.

5. Measure the results.

6. Standardize the new process (if the problem is solved).

HOW IS STATISTICAL THINKING IMPLEMENTED?

Find an important, real problem that is within reach of your work group. Start small, but not so small that a success will have almost no consequences. Celebrate the wins.

Position Statistical Thinking as a means to an end, not the end itself. Focus on a process under the work group's control, and use the combined thinking of all group members to guide the improvement process.

Use principles of good meeting processes to facilitate group participation, capitalizing on diversity among individuals to bring out all their ideas. Where new tools must be learned, be sure to present them in a manner that recognizes a diversity of learning styles. Work to find barriers to implementation, using new management tools such as affinity mapping and the interrelationship digraph.

APPENDIX:
Practice Scenarios—
Things to Consider

There are no correct answers for the case studies. However, we offer the following for consideration when leading discussions on the case studies.

Where's the Beef

a) Can the use of Statistical Thinking help solve this problem? Why or why not?

Statistical Thinking can help understand and assess the many processes and examples of variation. Some of the processes include cattle raising, beef preparation, inspection, and the processes consumers use to choose their diets. Understanding which processes have the most impact on the situation, and whether the variation reported in the article is common cause or special cause would be a starting point. The scenario referred to changes in market share and quantities of beef eaten per person per capita. Are these common cause or special cause variation?

b) If so, how should the beef industry respond, using Statistical Thinking?

- Determine scientifically the variation in quality of the beef.
- Determine how to improve the processes to improve the consistency and quality of beef.
- Use Quality Function Deployment (QFD) to identify the change in customers' needs.
- Consider a consumer education program.

- Compare the poultry and beef processes to identify whether the poultry process really does produce a more consistent product.
- Change the market strategy. Understand customers' needs and their decision processes.
- Understand the variation in customers.

Golden Acres

a) How could Statistical Thinking have been used to prevent this situation?

- Is the problem common cause or special cause? What about the solution?
- What processes and systems are at work?
- Consider variation in patient needs.
- Collect data before issuing a federal mandate.

b) How can Statistical Thinking be applied now to address the problem?

- Identify needed treatment for each patient.
- What data might be useful?
- Deal with special causes as though they are individual cases.

Right Illness, Wrong Prescription

a) How do you think Ben should approach this problem, using what he has just learned?

With a group of doctors, pharmacists and pharmacy assistants involved with the situation:

- Develop an operational definition for "inaccurate prescriptions."
- Look at prescription filling as a system of interconnected processes.
- Flowchart the process (system).
- Do a cause-and-effect analysis of inaccurate prescriptions.

- Agree on some actions that will improve the process.
- Agree on a set of metrics by which the accuracy of the prescription process can be measured.

  Follow up the meeting by

- Eliminating the obvious problems.
- Monitoring the process by charting the metrics over time.
- Identifying and eliminating special causes as they occur.
- Working with those involved in the system to improve it if the level of inaccurate prescriptions continues to remain at an unsatisfactorily high level.

Sales Rep of the Year

a) What assumptions is Ron making in his interpretation of the data?

- Percentage comparisons of two data points provide valid analysis.
- Every change is a special cause, and dealing with each situation individually can result in improved sales.
- Each region should perform the same way.
- Head-to-head competition among the sales reps will improve sales.

b) What questions should Ron ask?

- How can those managers with special-cause increases in sales teach the others?
- What is the market doing? How are we doing with respect to the changes?
- Are we losing market share?
- What do the customers want that we aren't providing?
- What's the nature of the business?
  - growing/achieving? (do they have the right data?)
  - market share by region?
- How long has each sales rep been in their region?
- What is the product mix?

c) What is the correct interpretation of the data?

When answering this question, consider the following:

- Plot the data by quarter for each region to look for trends, or stability.
- Examine for patterns (may differ by region).
- What is the normal quarter-to-quarter variation (from a moving range chart)?

Other observations and ideas that would be useful for Ron include:

- The sales force is not working together due to Ron's competitiveness.
- Meetings are only called when problems exist. They have no agenda and sales reps have no time to plan for the meeting. Perhaps they should meet more often for better communication and to work on their system.
- Sales goals are not defined.
- Define the interconnected processes involved in generating sales.
- Look at both unit sales and dollar volume.
- Consider other metrics—market share, per capita sales, etc.
- Define department goals—optimize the whole process.
- Optimize the whole company's result, not each region separately.

References

American Society for Quality Statistics Division (1996). *Glossary and Tables for Statistical Quality Control.* Milwaukee, WI: ASQC Quality Press.

Balestracci, D. (1998). *Data Sanity: Statistical Thinking Applied to Everyday Data.* Milwaukee, WI: American Society for Quality Statistics Division. Available from the Quality Information Center, American Society for Quality, PO Box 3005, Milwaukee, WI 53201-3005, 800-248-1946. Publication number S08–08.

Bernstein, R. K., M.D. (1984) *Diabetes: the GlucograF Method for Normalizing Blood Sugar,* Jeremy P. Tarcher, Inc., Los Angeles.

Box, G. E. P., Launer, R. L., and Wilkinson, G. N. (Eds.) (1979). Robustness in the Strategy of Scientific Model Building. *Robustness in Statistics.* New York: Academic Press, 201–236.

Box, G. E. P., Hunter, W. G., and Hunter, J. S. (1978). *Statistics for Experimenters.* New York: John Wiley and Sons.

Brassard, M. and Ritter, D. (1994). *The Memory Jogger II.* Methuen, MA: GOAL/QPC.

Britz, G., Emerling, D., Hare, L., Hoerl, R., and Shade, J. (1996). *Statistical Thinking.* Milwaukee, WI: American Society for Quality Statistics Division. Available from the Quality Information Center, American Society for Quality, PO Box 3005, Milwaukee, WI 53201-3005, 800-248-1946. Publication number S07–07.

Britz, G., Emerling, D., Hare, L., Hoerl, R., and Shade, J. (1997). How to Teach Others to Apply Statistical Thinking. ASQ *Quality Progress, 30* (June), 67–79.

Deming, W. E. (1982). *Out of the Crisis.* Cambridge, MA: MIT Center for Advanced Engineering Studies.

Doyle, M. and Straus, D. (1976). *How to Make Meetings Work.* New York: Jove Books.

Gaudard, M., Coates R., and Freeman L. (1991). Accelerating Improvement, ASQC *Quality Progress, 24* (October), 81–88.

Gunter, B. (1989). The Use and Abuse of C_{pk}. ASQC *Quality Progress, 22* (January), 72–73; (March), 108–109; (May), 79–80; (July), 86–87.

Gunter, B. (1991). The Use and Abuse of C_{pk} Revisited. ASQC *Quality Progress, 24* (January), 90–94.

Hahn, G. J., Hill, W. J., Hoerl, R. W., and Zinkgraf, S. A. (1999). The Impact of Six Sigma Improvement. *The American Statistician, 53* 3 (August), 1–8.

Hahn, G. J. and Meeker, W. Q. (1991). *Statistical Intervals.* New York: John Wiley and Sons.

Hare, L, Hoerl, R., Hromi, J., and Snee, R. (1995). The Role of Statistical Thinking in Management. ASQC *Quality Progress, 28* (February), 53–60.

Hoerl, R. and Snee, R. (1995). *Redesigning the Introductory Statistics Course.* (Technical Report No. 130). Madison, WI: Center for Quality and Productivity Improvement, University of Wisconsin.

Hoerl, R. and Snee, R. (2000). *Statistical Thinking For Business Improvement.* Pacific Grove, CA: Duxbury Press.

Hoffer, E. (1973). *Reflections on the Human Condition,* New York, Harper & Row ix, 97 p. 2cm.

Imai, M. (1986). *Kaizen, The Key to Japan's Competitive Success.* New York Random House Business Division.

Joiner, B. (1994). *Fourth Generation Management.* New York: McGraw-Hill.

Kepner-Tregoe Inc. (1979). *Problem Analysis and Decision Making.* Princeton NJ: Princeton Research Press.

Mager, R. (1988). *Making Instruction Work.* Belmont CA: Lake Publishing.

McCarthy, B. (1988). *4Mat Cycle of Learning,* Barrington, IL: EXCEL, Inc.

R. L. Launer and G. N. Wilkinson. "Robustness in the Strategy of Scientific Model Building," In *Robustness in Statistics,* eds, Academic Press, NY, 201–236.

Scholtes, P. R., Streibel, B, Joiner, B. L. (1996). *The Team Handbook.* (2nd ed.). Oriel, Inc., Madison, WI.

Shewhart, W. A. (1931). *Economic Control of Quality of Manufactured Product.* Republished by American Society for Quality Control, Milwaukee, WI, 1980.

Shewhart, W. A. (1939). Statistical Method from Viewpoint of Quality Control. Republished by Dover Publications, NY, 1986.

Section on Survey Research Methods, American Statistical Association. *What Is a Survey* series, ten pamphlets to date, Fritz Scheuren, Overall Series Editor, scheuren@aol.com. Single copies of each pamphlet are free by calling the ASA office at 703-684-1221.

Senge, P. (1990). *The Fifth Discipline.* New York: Doubleday/Currency.

Snee, R. D. (1986). In Pursuit of Total Quality. ASQC *Quality Progress, 19* (August), 25–31.

Wheeler, D. and Chambers, D. (1992). *Understanding Statistical Process Control.* (2nd ed.). Knoxville, TN: SPC Press.

Xerox Corporation (1993). *A World of Quality: The Timeless Passport.* Rochester, NY: Xerox Corporation, Xerox Quality Solutions.

Index